Ronald
REAGAN

Ronald REAGAN

JANICE ANDERSON

Optimum Books

Photographic acknowledgments

Frank Driggs, New York 14, 35, 53 bottom, 54; Flashbacks, London 8, 28, 60 top, 63, 65 bottom; Keystone Press Agency, London 13, 17, 18 left; Kobal Collection, London 11, 12, 15, 18 right, 19 bottom, 21, 22, 23, 26 top, 29 top, 29 bottom, 30 top, 30 bottom, 31, 32, 33, 34 top, 34 bottom, 36 bottom, 37, 40, 41 top, 41 bottom, 42, 43, 44 top, 44 bottom, 45, 46, 47, 48 top, 48 bottom, 49, 50, 51, 53 top, 55, 56 top, 56 bottom, 58, 59, 60 bottom, 62 top, 62 bottom, 64 top, 64 bottom, 65 top, 76–77, 78 bottom; Popperfoto, London 27, 61, 68, 70, 78 top; Rex Features, London 7, 9 top, 9 bottom, 16, 19 top, 20, 25, 26 bottom, 36 top, 38, 39, 52, 57, 66, 67, 69, 71, 72–73, 74, 75, 79; John Topham Picture Library 6.

Front cover: Rex Features.
Back cover: *Tropic Zone* (Paramount). Kobal Collection.
Frontispiece: Rex Features.

This edition published by Optimum Books 1982

Prepared by .
The Hamlyn Publishing Group Limited
London . New York . Sydney . Toronto
Astronaut House, Feltham, Middlesex, England

Copyright © The Hamlyn Publishing Group Limited 1982

ISBN 0 600 37794 6

Printed in Italy

CONTENTS

THE MAKING OF AN ALL-AMERICAN BOY

Ronald Reagan had a perfectly ordinary American upbringing: the sort of upbringing – quiet, unremarkable and based, despite his Catholic father, on solid White, Anglo-Saxon-Protestant virtues and on the belief that one man is as good as another – which leads every ordinary, warm-blooded American male to believe he can be President of the United States, or maybe a leading man in the movies, or at the least a college football star.

Ronald Wilson Reagan managed to be all three, which makes him a very remarkable man indeed.

His beginnings were unremarkable enough. He was born in the American mid-West, in the small town of Tampico, Illinois, on 6 February 1911. His father, Jack Reagan, was a first-generation American of Catholic Irish origin. His mother, Nelle, a Protestant, could claim Scots and English blood in her veins.

Now that their son is President of the United States and famous, the lands of his origins have also brushed up their relics of his forefathers, naming a pub after him in Tipperary and cleaning up the graves of the O'Regans in the churchyard at Ballyporeen, which Reagan's great-grandfather, Michael O'Regan, is thought to have left to escape the terrible potato famine of the mid-nineteenth century, which drove so many Irish across the sea to the United States. In England, the village where Nelle's family came from also takes pride in publicizing the fact.

All of which would have considerably surprised Ronald Reagan's parents. Jack Reagan was, most of the time, a shoe salesman who earned sufficient to ensure that the family, which included Ronald's two-years-older brother, Neil, was never exactly poor during his sons' childhood, though it was never well off, either. He was a good Democrat with a fine Irish sense of humour who believed in fighting fair, when you had to fight, and whose major weakness was an over-fondness for whisky.

Nelle Reagan was a quieter person, of perhaps more rigid principles; she was against drink, and although she never held Jack's problems with alcohol against him, she instilled in her sons a wariness of the stuff which Ronald has never lost. It was Nelle, perhaps more than Jack, who encouraged Ronald's interest in literature and acting. She herself loved books, read constantly to her children until they could read for themselves, and used to hold literary readings in the house. If there were a suitable play on in town, she would take her sons to see it.

At school, Ronald was an above-average pupil who read and studied a lot without ever becoming a swot and played as much sport as he could, especially football. Baseball was never on, for the short-sighted Reagan could not get his eye on the ball quickly enough.

It is not surprising, and indeed it seems like particularly happy type-casting, that two of Reagan's best film roles were to be sporting ones. In *Knute Rockne – All American* he had a big success as footballer George

In the graveyard of this church, the Church of the Assumption in Ballyporeen, Ireland, is an O'Regan family grave. Ronald Reagan's great-grandfather, Michael O'Regan, left the area after the potato famine.

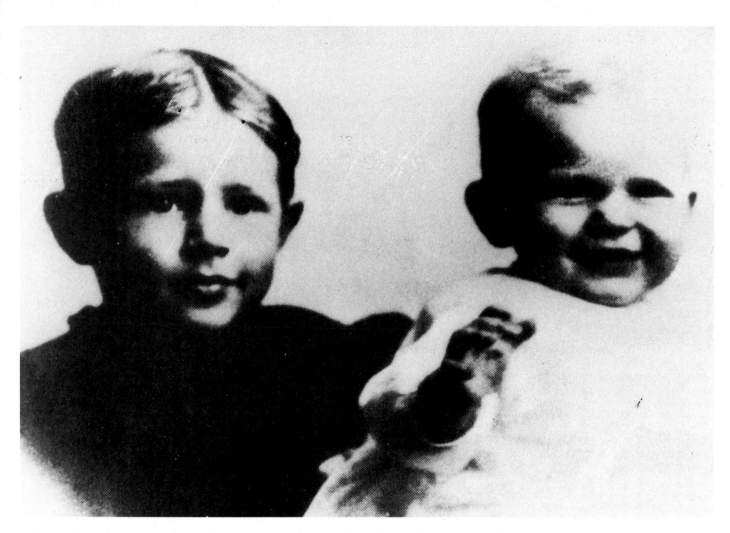

Gipp – the Gipper – and in *The Winning Team* his playing of pitcher Grover Cleveland Alexander won him the admiration of baseball fans all over the country. It was probably his performance as Alexander as much as his position as President of the US which led to Reagan's being invited to pitch the first ball of the US baseball National League's 1981 season at Cincinnati on 9 April; in the event, the President could not make it – he was recovering from a bullet wound in Washington State Hospital.

Reagan's early years were spent moving about from town to town as his father went after jobs, until they finally settled down in Dixon, 90 miles from Chicago. Here Reagan lived from the age of nine until he was 21. In the town's theatre he could glory in the activities of the early movie action men like Tom Mix and William S. Hart and was introduced to many plays, some good, some bad but all increasing the boy's interest in acting.

He also played football as much as he could, at high school and out of it, though the need to help with the family finances and save money for his college education meant that he had to start taking summer jobs at the age of 14, first with a construction company and then as a lifeguard. He had always been a good swimmer, so it seemed a reasonable enough way to earn money.

He was only a lad of 15 when he first became a lifeguard at Lowell Park, one of Dixon's two big recreational areas, and which was bordered by the Rock River where the swimming could be difficult. He loved the job and kept it for seven summers, during which he grew from a stripling into a fine young man, good looking with clean-cut features, an attractive smile and a fine physique. You would think that people, especially girls, would have been delighted to have been saved from drowning by such a fine example of all-American youth. Not so. According to Reagan, in his autobiography, 'Where's the Rest of Me?' (Elsevier-Dutton, New York, 1965) no one he hauled out of the Rock River ever thanked him; rather, they were annoyed that he should have made them look foolish in order, so they said, to make himself look heroic. Maybe he should have left the older people to look after themselves and stuck to rescuing damsels in distress, or to giving the kids swimming lessons.

The young Ronald Reagan (right), with his two-years-older brother, Neil.

7

himself winning an individual acting award. Not for the only time in his early life, he was asked if he had ever considered acting as a career: clearly, the talent was there.

Even politics came into his college life, in the form of a well-organized students' strike against proposed changes in the college's academic courses. Reagan took an active part, and found the whole business very much to his taste.

From college, where he graduated Bachelor of Arts, Reagan went into radio, landing a full-time job early in 1933. In those days, when Broadway or Hollywood both seemed as far away and inaccessible as the moon, radio was a pretty reasonable alternative for someone with show business aspirations – a branch of show business in which a local boy, if he were lucky, could make good.

And Reagan did make good. After a few preliminary disappointments, he was taken on as a radio announcer by radio station WOC in Davenport, Iowa, then moved to the bigger WHO Des Moines, Iowa, as a sports commentator. Reagan was lucky, too, for even at that local level, breaking into radio was not easy. Perhaps it was the luck of the Irish, or maybe Reagan's great grandfather, Michael O'Regan, had kissed the Blarney Stone and passed on the famous Irish 'gift of the gab' to his descendant, for young Reagan discovered within himself a gift for commentating fluently on sporting events, ad-libbing where necessary, and painting in words a picture of the scene which brought the whole thing vividly to life for the listeners at home.

Reagan was on a sports commentating assignment in Hollywood in 1937 when he got his first chance to become a film actor. It was the only chance he needed. On the evidence of one screen test, arranged by a Hollywood agent to whom he was introduced by a girl singer he knew from her early days on radio WHO Des Moines, Reagan was offered a seven-year contract with Warner Brothers. Within days of arriving on the Warners lot in June 1937, he was playing the lead in his first movie, *Love Is on the Air*. It was type-casting – he played a radio announcer – and it was a B movie, but still he was on his way. It all seemed remarkably easy.

It must have seemed great fun, too. Warners put out dozens of B movies, most of them intended to fill the first half of a double-feature programme and keep the customers happy until the big feature was screened. They would be shot in a matter of three or four weeks with a minimum of fuss and bother and certainly no arguments about the artistic integrity or aesthetic values of the whole thing. For the actors, it was more than

Respectable billing for Ronald Reagan in a poster for what was one of his best films, and one of his best roles, as a footballer in *Knute Rockne – All American* (Warner Bros.). Reagan is the kicker, top right.

Reagan's college years were spent at Eureka College, a Christian Church College at Eureka, 20 miles or so from Peoria in southern Illinois. Like the female star of one of his later movies, *She's Working Her Way Through College*, Reagan had to earn his college fees. He was awarded a scholarship which helped, but he still had to wash dishes – though in a girls' dormitory which must have eased the strain – to make ends meet. He also played a lot of football, captained the swimming team, and carried on with the drama he had enjoyed so much in high school, taking part in several college productions, one of which came second in a famous one-act play contest for colleges, Reagan

just a 'take-the-money-and-run' business; they were apprentices learning their craft, and there was a lot to learn about the movie-making business, as Reagan found out. His acting experience in school and college helped, though, and he was an apt pupil, discovering that most of the people he worked with on the Warners lot were happy to advise and encourage a young newcomer.

There was not that much money in the business in the early days, either, with the contract players expected to provide their own costumes at their own expense. A part requiring a dozen or so changes of costume could put a strain on a young man whose wardrobe ran to only four suits.

In 'Where's the Rest of Me?' Reagan remarked that, nearly 30 years later, he still stood in awe of actors who were said to possess wardrobes containing dozens of suits. Since then, times they have changed, and the current President of the United States is reported to buy his suits a dozen at a time, at $2000 or so per suit, from Beverly Hills' most expensive tailor. He would probably say, with some justification, that the script calls for them.

'B' MOVIE ACTION MAN

Between June 1937, when Ronald Reagan first became a contract player for Warner Brothers, until mid-1943, when he made his last commercial film until after the war, he played in 31 movies, and in at least one other film there was a part which ended up on the cutting room floor.

Thirty-two films in six years would not be a bad work record for any actor, but the speed with which they were turned out suggests that they were not all strongly budgeted, carefully planned and executed A features. In fact, many of them were B movies, Reagan himself admitting that Warners turned him into a sort of B movie Errol Flynn, playing parts which required plenty of dare-devil action and not too much serious acting. He spent a lot of time in those six years playing crusading radio announcers (surprise, surprise!) and newspaper reporters whose scoops would turn the town upside down, or secret agents fighting baddies in such exotic locations as prisons, dirigibles, aeroplanes and even a tugboat, or – more prosaically – insurance clerks and social workers.

There were parts in glossy A features in these years, and several more films were better than mere programmers, but the Reagan persona never seemed quite strong enough to make the star quality grade.

Perhaps his image was too much that of the basically nice guy, genial, good-humoured and on the whole pleasant to be with. He could not project the underlying sense of danger which made the Humphrey Bogarts or James Cagneys of the screen so attractive to audiences, he was not handsome enough to become another Robert Taylor, he lacked the charismatic charm of an Errol Flynn or a Clark Gable and his acting was generally just competent, so that no one could see in him another Spencer Tracy. On the other hand, he never enacted terrible scenes on set or refused roles in fits of ego-centric rage. He always turned up on time, knew his lines, and gave performances that were intelligently thought out and fitted in well with the general atmosphere of the story. Thus he was never out of work.

The 26-year-old Reagan stepped straight into the leading man category with *Love Is on the Air* (1937). He was Andy McLeod, a small-town radio announcer with a mission: to break up a crime syndicate which involved some of the local politicians and business-men. Downgraded to the kiddies' pro-gramme for mis-using air time to make his insinuations about criminals in high places, Andy encounters the love interest in the story – Jo Hopkins (June Travis) who backs him in his efforts. The denouement involves that fine old cliché, the confession by vil-lains who do not realize they are being overheard – this time by a radio audience listening in to Andy's programme.

The story was a re-hash on an old Paul Muni vehicle, *Hi Nellie!* (1934) in which the great Warners' actor, as a change from being a scarfaced gangster or a fugitive from a chain gang, played a campaigning newspaper re-porter reduced to the ranks of the lonely hearts column as punishment for being too outspoken in the columns of his employers' newspaper.

Love Is on the Air was shot in three weeks, and the edited version took up less than an hour's screen time, an indication of its sec-ond feature standing. Perhaps it was an in-dication, too, that Warners were not yet looking on their new recruit as a likely can-didate for the ranks of the big-time stars.

Reagan's next feature role was also in a B film, *Sergeant Murphy* (1938). Once again, the casting was appropriate, putting Reagan in the US cavalry and allowing him to show off his riding skills. His was not the title role; that belonged to a horse, a brilliant jumper who, in the film, eventually made it to England to cover himself in glory as the winner of the world-famous Grand National steeplechase. Santa Anita racetrack in Cali-fornia stood in for the famous Aintree course, which did not fool anyone who knew either course, and Ronald Reagan, in cavalry uniform or colourful racing silks, stood in for James Cagney, who had cleverly rejected the role when he read the script.

In the film, Reagan played cavalry private Dennis Murphy whose belief in a horse

Reagan got into *Swing Your Lady* (Warner Bros.) but his role was so small he could not get into the stills as well. The film was hardly kinder to star Humphrey Bogart (centre), who did not allow the film to get into his accounts of his career.

which seemed quite unsuitable for the cavalry because it could not be disciplined to remain quiet and controlled under the sound of gunfire, led him to acquire the animal for himself and train it for racing. He was helped in the task by the post Colonel's daughter Mary Lou Carruthers (Mary Maguire; Donald Crisp played her father, the Colonel). Eventually, the horse showed his true brilliance by winning the National, and private Murphy won the colonel's daughter, to the satisfaction of all, including – probably – the audiences for whom the film was, if nothing outstanding, at least a well-made study of horses and horse-racing, with action sequences which looked genuinely exciting.

From this film, having done a week's filming for a small role in a Pat O'Brien/George Brent navy movie, *Submarine D-1* which did not appear at all in the finished version, Reagan went into a so-called comedy, *Swing Your Lady*. Its star, Humphrey Bogart, preferred to forget to mention it in later accounts of his career, which is not surprising because it was not very good. It was supposed to be an uproarious farce, but the story was too unlikely even for that.

Bogart played Ed Hatch, a city sports promoter down on his luck in a small hillbilly town in Kentucky. The local blacksmith turned out to be a lady – or, at least, a female – called Sadie Horn (Louise Fazenda) and Ed Hatch conceived the happy notion of promoting a wrestling match between her and his last remaining property, a wrestler called Joe Skopapoulous (Nat Pendleton). Ronald Reagan hung around in the offing as a local

sports reporter by the name of Jack Miller.

In the end, nothing so distasteful as a wrestling match between the sexes was seen on the American screen for the story gave the lady blacksmith a boyfriend who took umbrage at the whole idea and ended up taking part in a wrestling match with Joe himself.

While the film did little for his standing as a movie actor, it at least gave Reagan some more experience and allowed him to get to know one of Warners' great stars. As it turned out he was to get plenty of experience in 1938, being given roles in another six films after *Swing Your Lady*.

He was back in the lead again in *Accidents Will Happen* as assurance adjuster Eric Gregg in the nasty position of being framed by his own wife (Sheila Bromley). The basis of the film's plot was a type of crime becoming all too prevalent in late 1930s America: the mounting of fraudulent claims against insurance companies. Nice honest Eric Gregg, having lost his job through his wife's misuse of his accounts, gets friendly with the sweet young thing (Gloria Blondell) who runs the cigar stand he patronizes and she supports and actively helps him in his schemes to vindicate himself and nail the villains of the piece. He succeeds in both aims, of course, and all ends well.

The Reagan seesaw dropped again after this, and he found himself half way down the cast list in his next film, *Cowboy from Brooklyn*. Heading the list, though, were Pat O'Brien and Dick Powell, the latter seeking recognition as an actor able to do more than sing pleasantly in musicals, plus the delightful Priscilla Lane, so it was an enjoyable film for Reagan to work on.

The plot revolves round the accidental way in which a city bumpkin, terrified of any sort of animal life, is transformed into a singing cowboy on radio by two smart operators from the world of show business. Dick Powell plays Elly Jordan, the 'cowboy' terrified of horses and Pat O'Brien is the smart operator, Roy Chadwick, who with his associate Patt Dunn (Reagan), turns the singer into a cowboy radio star. All goes well until people not unnaturally begin demanding that Elly should make personal appearances at horse shows, rodeos and the like. On horseback, of course. Help arrives in the form of Priscilla Lane as a rancher's daughter who just happens to be adept at hypnosis and she sets to work to help poor Elly. On the whole, she is successful, though there are occasions when Elly snaps out of the brave, horse-loving trance into which she has put him . . .

All ended happily, of course, but it was not the funny satire it might have been on

the school of cowboy songsters which Roy Rogers and Gene Autrey were to popularize, largely because poor Dick Powell just looked silly and embarrassed in his role. From Reagan's point of view, according to his autobiography, the best part about the film was working with and becoming friends of the film's two stars.

James Cagney did not turn down the lead role in Reagan's next film, *Boy Meets Girl*, which was an enjoyable film version of a Broadway success about Hollywood written by Sam and Bella Spewack. Pat O'Brien was also in this one, he and Cagney playing a pair of fast-talking, wacky screen-writers in a movie which, behind the comedy, managed to make some very sharp comments on the way in which the Hollywood studio system worked.

Reagan did not appear till the final reel, where he turned up as the radio announcer describing the scene outside the Carthay Circle Theater, a genuine Los Angeles landmark of the time, where a film premiere was taking place amidst the usual Hollywood publicity circus and floodlit ballyhoo.

A showcard for *Cowboy from Brooklyn* (Warner Bros.) showing Dick Powell practising being at home on a horse and Reagan looking as if not sure how to react to such nonsense.

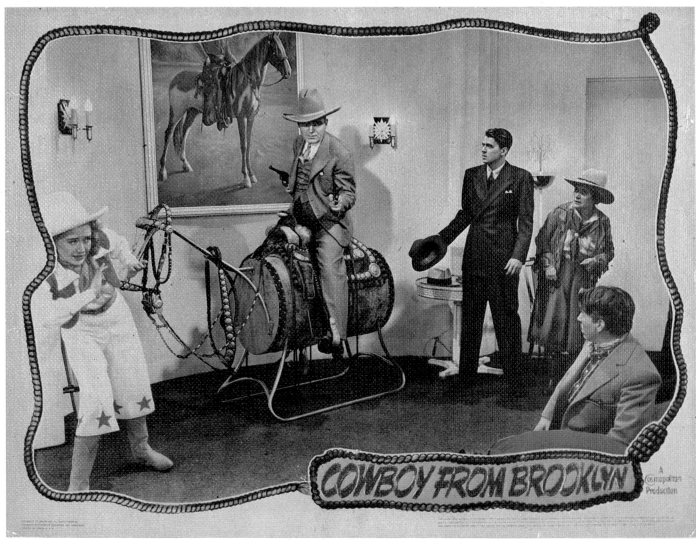

Once again, the film did not offer Reagan much of a chance to flex his muscles or demonstrate any ability to widen his range, but at least he was deepening his acquaintance with O'Brien and Cagney, both of them with the same Irish antecedents as himself. He felt he was no longer a newcomer on the edge of things, but had been accepted into the charmed inner circle of the Warners lot where Cagney, at the time one of America's most popular movie stars, shone brightly in the firmament. He had even, as he notes proudly in his autobiography, been granted a seat at the special table in the commissary where the great ones gathered, as if in some club where the membership was limited and all but the most fortunate aspirants were blackballed.

Young Ronald Reagan seems to have been pretty sure from the outset that he would make some sort of a career for himself in Hollywood, for he had only been there a short time when his parents moved west to join him, setting up their home in Hollywood. Brother Neil joined them later, also carving out a career for himself in the Dream Factory town.

After the fun of *Boy Meets Girl*, Reagan was back in the lead in the B grade again, in an indifferent effort called *Girls on Probation* which has since become notable only because Susan Hayward got her first part of any note in it.

Making a change from all those radio announcer/newspaper reporter parts, Reagan plays a thrusting young lawyer in this one, getting an attractive girl off a false charge of theft with a suspended sentence. The girl, Connie (Jane Bryan), seems to have an unfortunate knack of getting herself into trouble with the law, for she is soon involved, all innocently, in a bank robbery, gets caught in the getaway car and is put on probation.

Ronald Reagan with Jane Bryan in *Girls on Probation* (Warner Bros.). Reagan was a lawyer and Jane Bryan his girlfriend and client. A pipe was a favourite early prop of the future President.

13

After this, she gets a job in the young attorney's office, neglecting to tell him she is on probation for the bank robbery. Naturally, the two fall in love, but Connie's future is threatened when the friend who had mixed her up with the bank robbery turns up, the intention blackmail.

All ended happily, of course, not that anyone cared very much, for the script was poor, the direction anything but firm-handed, and the cast less than enthusiastic.

Reagan was lucky after this to get a really good part, in *Brother Rat* (discussed in the following chapter). It was his final film of a very busy year, and 1939 opened none too auspiciously with another minor part, this time in a Dick Powell vehicle, *Going Places*, distinguished only because Louis Armstrong sang in it that wonderfully lively Johnny Mercer/Harry Warren song 'Jeepers Creepers' (to a race horse, Jeepers Creepers, who would perform creditably on the race track only if sung to).

Reagan swanned through this one looking stylish in riding breeches, hacking jacket and cravat as the son of wealthy racehorse owner Colonel Withering (Thurston Hall), whose home is penetrated by Peter Mason (Dick Powell), a sports goods salesman hoping to interest the Colonel in his wares. In the event, he himself becomes interested in the Colonel's lovely daughter (Anita Louise).

Warners were being very frugal with this film, for it was the fourth time they had used the plot, originally a play called 'The Hottentot' by Victor Mapes and William Collier

Sr. Jerry Wald had a hand in the 1939 rewrite which turned out to be a bit of a plodder, despite the monied, horsey background to a plot which involved the hapless Dick Powell, unable to ride a horse, finding himself steering the cantankerous Jeepers Creepers, the Colonel's pride and joy, to victory in an important race.

Reagan enjoyed the horse scenes very much, especially the polo sequences. He was already moving in the horsy set of Los Angeles and was perhaps even thinking of the day when he would have his own ranch and breed his own horses.

If 1939 turned out to be anything special for Ronald Reagan it was not because of horses so much as because of the United States Secret Service. Warners had bought the film rights to the memoirs of a former head of the Service, William H. Moran, and decided to base a series of adventure films on his tales of the life of a secret agent, fighting baddies all over the world in order to preserve the American way of life. Warners gave the responsibility for using the material to Bryan Foy, head of their B pictures minor empire. Somewhere a scriptwriter came up with the splendid character Lieutenant Brass Bancroft, around whom a number of action-packed yarns, very loosely based on Moran's more sober tales, were woven, and Foy decided that the man to breathe life into the Bancroft character would be none other than Ronald Reagan.

Thus Reagan became an adventure film hero in the style of Buster Crabbe or Flash

A horsy Reagan in the horsy *Going Places* (Warner Bros.), trying to impress Anita Louise (left). Between them are Dick Powell, Minna Gombell and Rosella Towne.

SECRET SERVICE OF THE AIR

RONALD REAGAN
JOHN LITEL · ILA RHODES
JAMES STEPHENSON · EDDIE FOY, JR.

Directed by Noel Smith

PRESENTED BY

Warner Bros.

Gordon, thrilling the kids who filled America's cinema seats on Saturday afternoons with his splendid and romantic exploits. No one involved in these films saw in the young Reagan presidential material and, far from keeping him carefully wrapped in cotton wool, allowed him to do a lot of his own adventure stunts. More than once he ended a day's shooting covered in bruises from the thudding fists of the villain/stuntsman he had been fighting in front of the cameras. Once, he even stood like William Tell's son while a marksman knocked a bottle out of his hand with a slingshot: the course of history might have been changed if the stuntsman had turned out to be a very David and hit Reagan between the eyes.

Reagan was to make four Brass Bancroft movies in 1939 and 1940. The first was *Secret Service of the Air* in which Brass Bancroft, once in the army air corps and now earning a comfortable living as a commercial pilot, is inspired to throw it all away and join the

Secret Service, where the living, far from being easy, is dangerous in the extreme. The film also introduces audiences to Bancroft's side-kick, Gabby Watters, played by Eddie Foy Jr, who was to appear in all the Brass Bancroft films. Maybe just to confuse the kids in the audiences, Bancroft's boss, Saxby, was played by two different actors, John Litel and Joe King, in the course of the series.

In *Secret Service of the Air*, Brass Bancroft had the assignment of catching up with a particularly unpleasant gang of smugglers whose cargoes were human: aliens trying to enter the United States illegally. The smuggling was done in aircraft, and the film had some well-photographed aerial sequences.

In the next Brass Bancroft film, *Code of the Secret Service*, Reagan abandoned his flyer's leather jacket for costume more suited to hunting counterfeiters of American dollars in deepest Mexico. Somewhere along the line, the film's producers had also abandoned

A poster for *Secret Service of the Air* (Warner Bros.) shows Reagan in top billing as Brass Bancroft, a character he was to play in four movies in 1939 and 1940.

Reagan was to play with the Dead End Kids in a couple of films in 1939. This was the first, *Hell's Kitchen* (Warner Bros.), in which he was a social worker, here having a little trouble sorting out a dispute between Gabriel Dell and Leo Gorcey.

any pretensions to making a decent little movie, and the result was pretty dire. Reagan was so embarrassed by the edited film that he begged Warners not to show it within the Los Angeles boundaries.

Reagan made several other movies in 1939 before returning to his Brass Bancroft role for *Smashing the Money Ring*, also on the subject of counterfeiting. This time, the crooks were active in the United States, causing considerable alarm with the number of dud bills they were pushing out. To get himself in amongst the gang, Brass Bancroft set himself up as a counterfeiter, to the extent of being put in prison for his 'crimes'. Inside, he found that prison was providing the perfect cover for the gang, who were using the prison's own printing press to produce their forged bills.

The last Brass Bancroft film, *Murder in the Air* (1940), is also generally considered to be the best in the series. With one eye on the war in Europe, the concocters of this one turned it into a spy chase in which the future security of US aircraft in the air was jeopardized by the spy's scheme to steal the blueprints of a US Navy invention of a ray which could bring down aircraft several miles away. Highlight of the film was the scene in which a dirigible crashed into the sea.

However, 1939 was not all secret service stuff for Reagan. He had a bit part in yet

another Dick Powell musical, *Naughty but Nice*, the last the singing star was to make for Warner Brothers. In it, Powell was the naive and innocent backwoods professor of music trying to get his symphony published in New York. Naturally, he gets conned by many Tin Pan Alley sharks, but is fortunate enough to meet up with an angel fish, so to speak, in the form of honest music publisher Ed Clark (Reagan). By this time, one of the sharks has already pinched the theme of his great work for a song improbably called 'Hooray for Spinach', sung in the film, not by Popeye, but by Ann Sheridan, whom Warners were hoping to turn into a big star. Reagan does not mention the film in his autobiography.

Then there was the first of two films in which Reagan had to play with – or more correctly, in spite of – the notorious Dead End Kids, a group of kids from the slums of New York who had first been used to some effect in the Humphrey Bogart melodrama, *Dead End* (1937), and had since acquired a reputation for making life difficult for other actors who had to work with them.

The film was called *Hell's Kitchen* and in it Reagan had a below-the-title role as a social worker called Jim trying, with another social worker, Beth (Margaret Lindsay) to help run a shelter for the kids. The superintendent of the shelter, Crispin (Grant Mitchell) turns out to be a crooked operator. Fortunately for the kids and the shelter, the superintendent's assistant is an ex-racketeer with his heart in the right place (Stanley Fields) who manages, with the help of the Kids, to get rid of the Superintendent. There was not a lot for Reagan and Lindsay to do, apart from looking socially concerned and supportive, but they did supply the love interest, with their romance being given the blessing of the Dead End Kids.

From this Reagan, a glutton for punishment, went into his second Dead End Kids film, *Angels Wash Their Faces*, which, as the title makes obvious, was an attempt to cash in on the success of Cagney's hit of the year before, *Angels with Dirty Faces*. Cagney was nowhere to be seen in this one, and top billing went to Reagan, as Pat Remsen, the son of a district attorney, and to Ann Sheridan as Joy Ryan, sister of one of the Dead End Kids and Reagan's girl friend. Ann Sheridan had been in the original *Angels* film with Cagney; like Reagan, she seemed to have trouble in getting the message across to the Warner top brass that putting her into programmers after successful films was sending her career nowhere.

The plot revolved round the efforts of the Dead End Kids gang, called this time the Termites, to clear one of their number, Joy's brother, Gabe (Frankie Thomas) of a trumped-up charge of arson, efforts which were ultimately successful, of course.

Probably Reagan was not too bothered by the distinctly second-rate quality of these two films, if he even noticed it, for he had for some time been taken up with dating a pretty, blonde young Warners starlet, whom he had known since his earliest days on the Warners lot, but whom he did not begin taking seriously until they worked together in *Brother Rat* in 1938 (see following chapter).

The girl was Jane Wyman, and by 1939 they were officially engaged. The famous Hollywood columnist, Louella Parsons, liked them both and it was she who announced their engagement. She and her readers had good reason to think them a perfect couple, for they were both young, goodlooking and had about them the aura of being 'nice' as well. Publicity shots of the happy couple dining out in Hollywood showed him in the Gary Cooper image: pipe in hand, V-necked woollen sweater showing under tweed jacket, tie neatly knotted, thick wavy hair combed in place. Her style was elegant but restrained, with nothing flashy or over-made-up about her. Middle America loved them. Young America admired them too; in 1940 students at the University of California dubbed Ronald Reagan 'the 20th-century Adonis' and the sculpture students had him posing, football in hand, for their life class. Forty years later the world's press was to seize on this episode with glee because it allowed cheap jokes about 'ex-male model makes President,' or 'future President posed in his underpants'.

Ronald Reagan and Jane Wyman were married on 26 January 1940. Louella Parsons threw open her home for the wedding reception and provided a many-tiered wedding cake which towered above the newly-weds. The wedding photographs continued the 'nice young couple' image, with Reagan's parents, Nelle and Jack, beaming happily, flanking Mr and Mrs Ronald Reagan. The bride wore a full-length satin gown, a cute little fur hat with a net veil crowned her head, and one hand was thrust into a fur muff. Both Mrs Reagans wore large and opulent orchids and both Mr Reagans were attired in formal suits with dazzling white handkerchiefs showing in their breast pockets.

After the wedding, it was back to work for the newly-weds, though Jane Wyman was soon pregnant, their daughter Maureen being born a year, almost exactly to the day, after the wedding. Having adopted a boy, Michael, in 1945, the Reagans did have another daughter of their own but, tragically,

she was born four months premature in 1947 and lived only one day.

Perhaps this sad event had much to do with Jane Wyman asking Reagan for a divorce in 1948. She herself said that Reagan's deep involvement in local politics at this time with all the consequent talk about politics at the breakfast table eventually proved too much for her, and certainly there had never been any gossip about affairs with other people in either of their lives. Reagan himself has said little about the divorce, either in his autobiography, or elsewhere, contenting himself with remarking that it came upon him as a complete, and nasty surprise.

Reagan married Jane Wyman in January 1940. The reception was held at the home of the columnist Louella Parsons, who publicized them as an ideal American pleasant young couple.

Above: Reagan and Jane Wyman with their daughter Maureen Elizabeth in 1942, when Reagan was serving as a lieutenant in the US Cavalry.

Above right: The marriage of Ronald Reagan and Jane Wyman was apparently happy and gossip-free, but after six years she surprised him by asking for a divorce, claiming that politics was increasingly occupying his time.

Reagan's first post-marriage films in 1940 were nothing for film buffs to get excited about. There was a sequel to *Brother Rat* (with Jane Wyman also in the cast), his fourth Brass Bancroft saga, and *An Angel from Texas*, in which Jane Wyman also starred.

Eddie Albert and Wayne Morris had the leads in this one, Eddie Albert as the country-boy innocent, Peter Coleman, come to New York from Texas with $20 000 in his pocket, which he wants to sink into a hotel, and Wayne Morris as the theatrical producer, Mr McClure, intent on turning Coleman into an 'angel,' and thus obtain the financial

backing for his latest Broadway venture. Reagan was the producer's partner, Mr Allen, and Wyman was Mrs Allen.

Since Peter Coleman wants to see his girl-friend's name in lights on Broadway, the two producers do not find it too difficult to persuade him to part with his money for the play, a tense drama, since they agree to cast her in the lead. This causes a small hiccough in the smooth running of events, as the producers have already offered the part to someone else, and she threatens to put the heavy mob on them if she does not get it. Eventually, the play goes ahead with Coleman's girlfriend Lydia (Rosemary Lane) playing the lead. The production is so dreadful that the drama becomes a farce, audiences love it, the box-office takings mount satisfactorily, and everyone is happy – except, perhaps Mr George S. Kaufman, author of the original Broadway play, 'The Butter and Egg Man', of which *An Angel from Texas* was the fourth, rather feeble screen version.

Even when Reagan was given parts in A feature films in 1940, such as *Knute Rockne*

Left: In *An Angel from Texas* (Warner Bros.) Reagan was partner to a theatrical producer, Wayne Morris (left), and Rosemary Lane (right) was trying to make Broadway. Jane Wyman (centre), Reagan's wife, was also his wife in the movie.

– *All American* and *Santa Fe Trail*, Warners still chose to push him back down towards the B ratings, or at least, the shaky As, in between, rather than finding anything better for him to do. It was not as if they were making sure that he really worked for his contract artist's regular wage packet, for *Tugboat Annie Sails Again* took only three weeks or so to shoot, leaving Reagan and Jane Wyman, who also had a part in this movie, plenty of time to play the happy newly-weds on the Hollywood social scene. *Tugboat Annie Sails Again* was not a bad film, exactly; it just lacked the sheer joy for life and the perfectly-timed comedy which Marie Dressler and Wallace Beery had communicated so well in the original MGM film, *Tugboat Annie* (1933). Warners had acquired the rights to the Tugboat Annie character which Norman Reilly Raine had created, but unfortunately they did not have a Marie Dressler to play her, nor did they use Wallace Beery to play again the role of her ne'er-do-well husband, choosing rather to cut him out of the new plot altogether. Marjorie Rambeau was Annie, and seemed rather good in the part provided you could not remember Marie Dressler playing it. Reagan played Eddie King, Annie's young sailor protégé who was poor but honest, and Jane Wyman was Peggy Armstrong, a wealthy young woman who falls in love with Eddie.

The plot centred round Annie's efforts to keep her tug, *Narcissus*, in business in a busy West Coast port against the competition of other tugboat owners, notably one Captain Bullwinkle, played by Alan Hale. Much of

Reagan and Marjorie Rambeau in *Tugboat Annie Sails Again* (Warner Bros.), in which Marjorie Rambeau played Annie, the role made famous in an earlier film by Marie Dressler. Reagan was Annie's young protégé in a film which failed to capture the style of the Dressler-Wallace Beery classic.

the film was shot on location in Los Angeles' port, which made a pleasant break for all concerned in the filming.

The year 1941 opened with another less than satisfactory part for Reagan, as Lionel Barrymore's nephew Gil Jones in *The Bad Man*, made at Metro. This was Reagan's first loan out from Warners, and it was something of an eye-opener for him to see the lavish way in which MGM went about making their movies, when compared with the careful cheese-paring that was very much the order of the day back at the Warner lot.

Reagan was hired to MGM to be the young lead in the film, but in fact he had little chance of doing anything except hang around – almost literally in one scene – in a film which had Wallace Beery scene-stealing outrageously as Lopez, the Bad Man and a Mexican border bandit with a heart of gold, and Lionel Barrymore charging about in a wheelchair trying to raise the mortgage money to keep his ranch from being snatched from him. Eventually, Lopez comes to the rescue, saving young Gil from a bandit's noose, and finding the money to allow Gil's uncle to pay off the mortgage. He also manages to arrange things so that Gil's boyhood sweetheart Lucia (Laraine Day) is freed from her boring husband so that she and Gil can make a twosome of it.

It might not have been the world's greatest movie, but Reagan enjoyed working with Beery, Barrymore and the 'very nice' Laraine Day.

From *The Bad Man* and the Tiffanys of MGM, it was back to the meat and potatoes of Warners, as Reagan put it, to star in *Million Dollar Baby* with Priscilla Lane, May

Robson and Jeffrey Lynn. Reagan played a pianist, Peter Rowan, in this one, and had to put in hours at the keyboard learning to play the piano – or, at least, to look as if he were playing the piano – in order to give a good account of the part of the struggling young concert pianist. In fact, Reagan was more than competent in this one, displaying a light touch with lines, and the whole thing turned out to be an enjoyable comedy.

The 'million dollar baby' of the title is Priscilla Lane, as Pamela McAllister, who receives, out of the blue, a gift of one million dollars from millionairess Miss Wheelwright (May Robson), ageing daughter of a man who, it now turns out, had made his fortune by defrauding Pamela's grandfather many years before. Miss Wheelwright is in Europe when young lawyer James Amory (Jeffrey Lynn) arrives to tell her the truth about the money which has been hers for so long. Appalled, Miss Wheelwright decides to return to America to see if there is anything she can do to make amends.

Once back in the States, Miss Wheelwright discovers Pamela living a blameless life in a small boarding house, moves in herself in order to discover more about the girl, and soon decides to give her a million dollars. This seems a very good thing to Pamela until her true love, the struggling young pianist, Peter, draws back from her, too sensitive to want to benefit from marriage to a rich girl. In the end, Pamela decides that Peter is more important to her than money, and gets him back by giving it all away to charity.

In the meantime, Miss Wheelwright is discovering how ordinary American people, who are not cushioned from the realities of life by the possession of vast sums of money, manage to make do – all of which is very salutary for her, and makes a nice sub-plot for the film, which was, in fact, based on a story 'Miss Wheelwright Discovers America' by Leonard Spigelglass.

Reagan's next film, *Nine Lives Are Not Enough*, was a real B movie of the old school, a short, swift-paced and entertaining programmer. Reagan was back in a familiar role, too, as keen young, hat-on-the-back-of-the-head newspaperman Matt Sawyer, not afraid to put his future on the line by writing a story which, while accusing a prominent citizen of being a gangster and racketeer, also put his newspaper on the receiving end of a libel suit.

This trouble results in Sawyer being moved off the main news team and on to the police beat, where it is not long before he is reporting an apparent case of suicide, committed by a local millionaire. Sawyer senses murder most foul and says so loud and clear in his newspaper. The coroner disagrees,

Reagan's first film away from Warner Brothers was *The Bad Man* for MGM, in which, playing the lead (but not the Bad Man), he found himself close to being suspended on the end of a rope.

Reagan should have looked right in *Nine Lives Are Not Enough* (Warner Bros.) for he was back in his old role of a newspaper man in an action-packed movie.

there is another argument, and this time Saw-yer loses his job altogether. By now, the reporter is like a terrier with a bone, refusing to give up his murder story, and investigates it more thoroughly, helped by the friends he has made in the local police department and by the dead millionaire's daughter, Jane (Joan Perry).

The action-packed movie ends with the suicide being proved indeed to be murder, the millionaire's business partner having done it to further his shady activities with the racketeer who figured in the story which had originally landed Sawyer in all his trouble. The millionaire's daughter, now wealthy herself, of course, and very much in love with the dashing Sawyer, buys up his

old newspaper and installs him in the editor's chair: love – and money – conquers all.

In total contrast was the story of *Juke Girl* (1942) in which Reagan starred once again with Warners' glamour girl, Ann Sheridan (the one with 'oomph'). This was a sort of sub-Steinbeck story of migrant crop pickers in Florida and there was precious little glamour about it. It was also a pretty poor thank-you to two actors who had just done such a good job for Warners in *King's Row* (see next chapter). The film offered a message of social concern: the conditions under which the farm workers lived and laboured were appalling and the film depicted their exploitation by monopolistic packing house owners who could dictate the prices – as low

'Oomph Girl' Ann Sheridan and Reagan had made a success of *King's Row* in 1942, but were then put into the poor *Juke Girl* (Warner Bros.) as migrant crop pickers. George Tobias is with them in this scene.

Not exactly the gates of the White House, and not the sort of picture to be found in the albums of many of the Presidents of the United States. Reagan, about 1943.

as possible – paid to farmers, with realistic violence.

Ann Sheridan came into the story as one of the girls employed in a juke joint to provide the field workers with some off-duty entertainment. The dreariness of her life was more than matched by that of Steve Talbot (Reagan), a drifter picking up work where he could, but the two sensed an affinity between them, and together joined the despairing workers in a last-ditch fight against the thugs of the packaging house management.

The occasion of the finale fight was a consignment of tomatoes which the farmers were sending off to the salesyards independently of the packagers, who naturally tried to stop them. In the inevitable brawl, the fighters found themselves knee-deep in tomatoes and using them as weapons. The fight took three cold, desperately uncomfortable nights to film, and the same truckloads of tomatoes were used throughout. The whole nightmarish episode put Reagan right off tomatoes for years.

INTO THE 'A' GRADE

Ronald Reagan's film career was never a major success story. Not for him the unswerving path to the top, with one picture after another adding to his reputation either as an actor or as a major star. The two things are not, of course, necessarily the same thing; there have been many fine actors who have never made it to star status in the cinema while, on the other hand, there have been many stars whose acting abilities could hardly be rated high. To give him his due, Reagan was never less than a competent actor, and after two or three years with Warners he was also generally recognized as one of Hollywood's leading young male stars, but that was about it.

His problem, if it could be called that, almost certainly lay within himself: he does not appear to have been consumed with the driving ambition necessary to get right to the top of the industry. He probably knew better than Warners what films were right for him and which ones would only lead to disaster, but at least in his early years he was not prepared to go out on a limb for them. He enjoyed his life in Hollywood, he was happy to earn a good enough salary to keep himself and his family in comfort, if not in luxury, and that was fine by him.

His career was not helped by the outbreak of the Second World War, either. He ended up in the army, out of the public eye for several years, thus allowing other young actors the chance to come along and fill the place he was beginning to carve out for himself.

Then there was Warner Brothers studio itself. Perhaps Reagan's career would have taken off more spectacularly if he had done the film test his agent arranged for him at Paramount at the same time as he took the Warners' test that led to his entry into Hollywood. Reagan had not bothered to stay in Hollywood to take the Paramount test, and had no hesitation in becoming a contract player at Warners, a studio not noted for the care it lavished on its contract artists.

Bette Davis, one of Warners' hardest working and most successful stars, who had more than one battle with them over parts, once said that whereas MGM treated their female stars like queens, Warners looked on theirs as factory workers. Olivia de Havilland made Hollywood history in the 1940s by taking Warners to court in a series of long and bitter fights to establish that no studio had the right to add extra months to a contract in order to get out of an actor time lost through suspension from the studio. She won, and seven years became the legal upper limit for a film contract, including time lost through suspension. Warners' male stars were treated no better, and perhaps it was his experience with them that made Ronald Reagan such a stalwart of the Screen Actors Guild (which had backed de Havilland in her fight with Warners) after the war.

All of this notwithstanding, Ronald Reagan did have good parts in good pictures during his pre-war years in Hollywood, one or two of which are even considered classics by film buffs.

His second screen appearance, though a very fleeting one, was in an undoubted A: *Hollywood Hotel*. This was Busby Berkeley's Christmas present to America in 1937 and was a frothy package of songs, romance and comedy, with Dick Powell and the Lane sisters, Lola and Rosemary, heading the cast. The seven Johnny Mercer/Richard A. Whiting songs included 'I've Hitched My Wagon to a Star' and 'Hooray for Hollywood', the words of which included a crack about Hollywood being the place where 'you're terrific if you are even good'.

Young Reagan was not given the opportunity to be good enough to be considered terrific. His name did not appear on the published cast list and his piece of the action was two and a half lines long: blink and you would miss it. He came on in the finale as a radio announcer standing beside that powerhouse of newspapers and radio, Louella Parsons. The film was based on the successful, nation-wide radio show of the same name in which Dick Powell, Louella Parsons and Frances Langford (also in the film) starred.

One year and half a dozen fairly indifferent films later, Reagan was given a starring

role in *Brother Rat*, a real, grade A comedy, and a big hit with American cinema audiences. The setting for this film was Virginia Military Institute, a genuine US military academy, and the story recounted the exploits of a group of the cadets there. The film was based on a hit Broadway play by John Monks Jr and Fred Finkelhoffe, in which the lead had been taken by an actor called Eddie Albert, then unknown in Hollywood.

He was brought West to recreate his stage role, Bing Edwards, for the film, though for this version the role was reduced in status to allow Wayne Morris to play the lead, cadet Billy Randolph, and to give Reagan the third starring role of cadet Dan Crawford.

The picture, whose title was taken from the nicknames the cadets had for each other (Reagan was 'Brother Mouse'), revolved around the high-spirited, not to say wild, activities of the trio. Billy and Dan, in particular, got up to some exceedingly hair-

raising antics (or so they were meant to seem to late 1930s' audiences) which would probably have had them thrown out of VMI on their ears had they been discovered. Bing, though less rowdy, had a problem which, if discovered, would certainly have led to expulsion: he was married, a condition expressly forbidden by VMI rules. What was worse, his wife was pregnant.

Bing's problem, and how to keep it secret, plus the efforts of all three cadets to get themselves academically and militarily into sufficient order to graduate, provided the complex plot with its basic outline. The cadets' efforts were complicated by their love lives, Dan Crawford living dangerously indeed by dating the commandant's vivacious, blonde daughter, Kate (Jane Wyman).

Reagan was good in *Brother Rat*, displaying a light, sure touch with the comedy. Unfortunately for him, Eddie Albert turned out to be even better and ran away with the whole film.

Brother Rat (Warner Bros.) was a comedy of the adventures of three cadet comrades at the Virginia Military Institute. Reagan (left) and Wayne Morris were two of them, and one of Reagan's escapades was dating the commandant's daughter, Jane Wyman (centre), whom he later married in real life.

25

Above: Bette Davis (right) was the star of *Dark Victory* (Warner Bros./First National), a typical tear-jerker in which she bravely faces a life threatened by a brain tumour. Reagan had a bit part which he later thought he played poorly.

Right: A scene from *Dark Victory* (Warner Bros./First National) in which Reagan loved the doomed socialite Bette Davis. Reagan's character was called Alec Hamm, an unfortunate name for a young actor finding himself supporting several big stars.

Because the film was a big success, Warners decided to do a follow-up, *Brother Rat and a Baby*, in 1940. As is often the way with sequels, this one was not a patch on the original, despite having much the same cast and the same writers, Jerry Wald and Richard Macaulay, to produce the script. The director was different, though, Ray Enright replacing the vastly experienced William Keighley, and perhaps it was the absence of Keighley's sure hand that made the comedy seem silly and even tiresome, rather than great fun.

After *Brother Rat* was completed, Reagan went back to bit parts or the B grade for his next couple of films. Then Warners offered him a small role in a Bette Davis tearjerker, *Dark Victory*.

There were so many good actors in this film that it is no wonder that Reagan seemed less effective than he might have been, though he did manage to turn his bit part into something of a cameo role. Heading the cast, the marvellous Bette Davis was able to pull out all the stops as a rich carefree young socialite, Judith Traherne, whose world was shattered when she discovered she had a brain tumour. The film traced the brave way she came to terms with her affliction so that she was able to face her approaching death with quiet courage.

Geraldine Fitzgerald had a good role as Judith's secretary and friend, Ann King, and George Brent had the difficult part of the brain specialist, Dr Frederick Steele, who diagnosed that Judith's days were numbered while at the same time he was falling in love with her. Even Humphrey Bogart was in the film, as Michael O'Leary, the trainer of Judith's thoroughbred horse; his big scene came when he had to try to persuade Judith that Dr Steele's proposal of marriage arose, not out of pity for her condition, but out of genuine love for her as a woman. Reagan's part was that of Alec Hamm, a rich young man, often drunk, who formed part of the court around Judith and who was also in love with her.

Talking about the film later, Reagan came to the conclusion that his own relative inexperience left him in no position to argue with the director, Edmund Goulding, about how his scenes should be played, and he eventually gave a reading which he considered to be wrong – and bad.

Be that as it may, it was to be some time before Reagan got another good role in an A film, but this time it was one of his best. It was a part he had wanted to play for some time and which he knew he could do well, that of legendary footballer George Gipp, the 'Gipper', in the biopic *Knute Rockne – All American* (1940).

Pat O'Brien played the title role, that of the Norwegian-born Knute, one of America's greatest footballers of all time, who also became coach to the famous Notre Dame university team. Reagan had to do a lot of hard talking and much displaying of his college football photos to the Warner production heads to get the role of the Gipper for himself, for the top brass did not consider he looked like a footballer. Eventually, he was tested, and was in.

It was not a long part, taking up only one reel of the film, but it was certainly effective. As Reagan said in 'Where's The Rest of Me?', it was a nearly perfect part, with a great entrance, an action middle and a death-

Reagan as a footballer in a film which earned him some celebrity, *Knute Rockne – All American* (Warner Bros.). Reagan played football hero George Gipp, and has been known as 'The Gipper' ever since.

In *Santa Fe Trail* (Warner Bros./First National), Reagan played the famous General Custer – but before the Big Horn massacre. Errol Flynn was the equally famous Jeb Stuart, supposedly a West Point comrade of Custer's, just one of the film's historical inaccuracies.

bed scene to finish (Gipp died tragically young of pneumonia). Finished, but not forgotten, for Pat O'Brien got one of his best lines ever near the end of the film when rallying his flagging Notre Dame team to one last winning effort, he shouted at them to 'win one for the Gipper!'.

Reagan had another enjoyable part later that year in the Errol Flynn/Olivia de Havilland movie *Santa Fe Trail* in which he played a liberal young soldier from West Point named George Armstrong Custer – yes, that one, though the massacre at Little Big Horn was years ahead of this particular story. The script, taking massive liberties with the true course of American military history, called for the famous Confederate cavalry commander, Jeb Stuart (Errol Flynn) to be a West Point comrade of Custer's, though in fact, they were years apart, and were on opposite sides in the Civil War. The film had little to do with the realities of the Santa Fe Trail either, being largely concerned with the abolitionist career of John Brown, he whose soul goes marching on (played, with a fanatical glint in his eye, by Raymond Massey). The climactic scene of the film was John Brown's hanging.

Reagan's role required him to be the victim of unrequited love – for Kit Carson Halliday (Olivia de Havilland), who was naturally marked out to be Jeb Stuart's partner in life. Before the film was over, Custer had found a love of his own, Charlotte, played by Susan Peters (billed in this film as Suzanne Carnahan).

With a good cast and plenty of action, and well directed by Michael Curtiz, *Santa Fe Trail* was assured of success and is, indeed, still an entertaining movie on television.

Reagan's next A role, and undoubtedly the best of his movie career, could hardly be described as 'entertaining'. He played a rich young layabout, Drake McHugh, fated to lose first his fortune then both his legs, in *King's Row* (1942).

This was an unusually adult and down-to-earth story of the often unpleasant goings-on and relationships in a small American town at the beginning of the century. Insanity, jealous love, death through cancer, and even a piece of medical sadism, all had their place in what could have been a pretty depressing tale, but which was saved from being so by the quality of its production and because of its optimistic ending.

In the story, Drake's loss of his legs turns out to have been unnecessary; he had been severely injured in an accident at the local railroad yard, and Dr Gordon (Charles Coburn), who amputated his legs, did so not because no other course was open to him, but because he wanted to punish the young man for his former loose ways: his daughter, Louise Gordon (Nancy Coleman) had once loved Drake, but he had turned from her, preferring the warmer company of the more outgoing Randy (Ann Sheridan).

The scene in which Drake McHugh awakes from his operation and slowly realizes that he has lost his legs was one of the most difficult of Reagan's acting career. He worried for weeks about how he was going to jump the biggest hurdle of the scene, speaking the line 'Where's the rest of me?' without making it sound trite. In the end, he managed it perfectly on the first take, and it remains a telling scene in the film.

The main reason why *King's Row* is a cinema classic is because Warners gave it the best of everything. The cast was splendid, including as it did Judith Anderson as Mrs Gordon, and Claude Rains, giving a fine performance as Dr Tower, father of the 'odd' and eventually hopelessly neurotic Cassandra (Betty Field), a childhood sweetheart of Drake's friend, Parris Mitchell, a part also given a fine reading by Robert Cummings. It is Parris, eventually finding happiness of his own, not with poor demented Cassandra but with a lovely young Viennese girl (Karen Verne), who persuades Drake that he must pick up the pieces of his life again, making a future for himself and Randy.

Sam Wood, who had been involved in direction since the days when he assisted Cecil B. de Mille during the silent movie days of the First World War, directed with skill and finesse; James Wong Howe, one of Hollywood's greatest cinematographers of all time, was behind the camera; and background atmosphere was superbly supplied by the music of Czech composer-prodigy, Erich Korngold.

Above: Reagan played with some of Hollywood's greatest stars. He looked a little puzzled as he plays gooseberry in *Santa Fe Trail* (Warner Bros./First National) while Errol Flynn makes eyes at Olivia de Havilland.

Left: There were good performances by all the principals in the excellent *King's Row* (Warner Bros.), in which picture Reagan lost his legs. Ann Sheridan was the girl he fell in love with and Robert Cummings his friend.

29

WAR MOVIE HERO

Far right: Reagan was in the US Cavalry in 1939, and an issue of *Modern Screen* contained an article called 'My Soldier' by his wife.

Bottom: In *International Squadron* (Warner Bros.), Reagan played a Yank who joined the RAF.

Below: The decor of Reagan's room in *International Squadron* (Warner Bros.) helped US audiences to get the picture.

When the Second World War began in Europe in 1939, Ronald Reagan was already a reserve officer in the US Cavalry. He had joined the cavalry in the mid-1930s largely because it had seemed an excellent place in which to learn about looking after horses and to get plenty of opportunities to ride them. The 14th Cavalry Regiment was stationed in Des Moines, where Reagan was working on radio WHO, so he joined them. He had to pull a trick or two to convince them that he could see perfectly without his glasses – which he could not – but he made it, and was soon a fine rider.

Once the United States entered the Second World War after Pearl Harbor, Reagan soon found himself inducted into the US Army, with the rank of second lieutenant in the cavalry. This was no bad thing, for it permitted some handsome publicity shots of the gallant officer looking dashing in riding boots and breeches, and gave Warners the opportunity to bill him as 'Lt Ronald Reagan' on their posters and lobby cards for one of his war-time films, *This Is the Army*.

As it turned out, Reagan's war was fought on home ground, for his shortsightedness disqualified him for combat duty. He was at Fort Dixon, San Francisco, as a liaison officer for a time, then was transferred to the Army Air Corps. From there, he was sent to the Hal Roach Studios in Culver City, California, where a vast number of training films, documentaries and war newsreels were churned out during the course of the War. Reagan acted in, narrated and directed training films, appeared in promotional films and also made personal appearances at war effort events. By the time he was discharged from the army in 1945, he had reached the rank of captain.

He was allowed time off his war service commitments to make movies – Hollywood's own contribution to the war effort and to the support of national morale. In fact, though eight of Ronald Reagan's films, apart from the two *Brother Rat* films, had him in modern service uniform, only three of them were made during the war.

The first of Reagan's war-time films in uniform was *International Squadron*, made in 1941 before the US had entered the war. Europe was well in the hellish grip of it all, however, so naturally enough the film had a European setting, or at least, a British one: the Royal Air Force.

In playing a cocky Yank who joins the RAF, Reagan was following in the footsteps of Tyrone Power, who played a similar role in *A Yank in the RAF*, also released in 1941. He was also following a trail blazed by James Cagney, for Reagan's movie, made by the 'count-every-penny' Warner Brothers, was based on the script of *Ceiling Zero* (1935) in

MODERN SCREEN

JANUARY

10 CENTS

JANE WYMAN
RONALD REAGAN

"MY SOLDIER" BY JANE WYMAN

OI303

On the door: NICHTBESCHÄFTIGTEN IST DER ZUTRITT VERBOTEN

NUR FÜR ANGESTELLTE

which Cagney had played a commercial pilot, finally atoning heroically with his own life for causing the death of a fellow pilot.

In *International Squadron*, Reagan plays a care-free stunt pilot, Jimmy Grant, who agrees to deliver a bomber to England for the RAF, where he finds a couple of his friends already in uniform and flying for the British. The sight of a child being killed during the Blitz in London makes Jimmy decide that the RAF, from where he could help fight the Germans, is also the place for him to be.

Once in uniform, he still does not take the war business very seriously, and even misses a bombing mission because he is more interested in Jeanette (Olympe Bradna), the charming young girlfriend of a French pilot. One of Jimmy's American friends stands in for him on the mission and 'fails to return'. Horrified that his irresponsible attitude has caused his friend's death, Jimmy atones by taking the French pilot's place on another dangerous mission, in the course of which he accounts heroically for several German planes before going down himself in a blaze of fire and glory.

It was all good, morale-boosting stuff, and Reagan played his part well, with a likeable and insouciant confidence, as he was to do in his next war movie, *Desperate Journey* (1942). Once again, he was in the RAF, though this time Errol Flynn was around to provide plenty of competition in the insouciant charm department. Flynn was the Australian pilot, Flight Lt Terence Forbes, of an RAF bomber and Reagan was the brave Yank, Flying Officer Johnny Hammond.

Seen today – and even at the time – *Desperate Journey*, which is all about how the remnants of the bomber crew, shot down over Europe, get back to England after a series of wildly improbable adventures, looks very unlikely *Boy's Own Paper* stuff. But director Raoul Walsh made sure the action was fast, and no doubt the kids in the back row enjoyed it as much as they had enjoyed Reagan's Brass Bancroft adventures, especially the scene in which Flying Officer Hammond, being interrogated by Nazi Major Otto Baumeister (Raymond Massey) while the latter eats his breakfast, takes a swing at the Major's jaw, knocks him out and helps himself to the breakfast.

Above: There were some improbable adventures for Reagan in *Desperate Journey* (Warner Bros./First National) in which, as an RAF officer shot down in Europe, he fought his way back to England to continue the good fight.

Far left: Reagan teamed up again with Errol Flynn in *Desperate Journey* (Warner Bros./First National). Alan Hale (left) was also in the movie, and the three were part of a bomber crew who would not allow their being shot down to prevent them waging the war.

Right: Irving Berlin provided the music for a blockbuster war propaganda film *This Is the Army* (Warner Bros.) for which Reagan was seconded from the army and the posters for which billed him as 'Lt. Ronald Reagan'.

Irving Berlin's
THIS IS THE ARMY
in Technicolor

GEORGE MURPHY · JOAN LESLIE
LT. RONALD REAGAN

GEORGE TOBIAS · ALAN HALE · CHAS. BUTTERWORTH

PRESENTED BY
WARNER BROS.
PRODUCED BY
JACK L. WARNER
and
HAL B. WALLIS

KATE SMITH and
MEN FROM THE
ARMED FORCES

DIRECTED BY MICHAEL CURTIZ

Distributed by Warner Bros. Pictures. Ltd   PRINTED IN ENGLAND

Below: *This Is the Army* (Warner Bros.) was a military version of the show-within-a-picture theme, and was based on a successful Broadway show. Reagan, as the producer of the show, is seen studying the script in which he rehearses his fellow-soldiers.

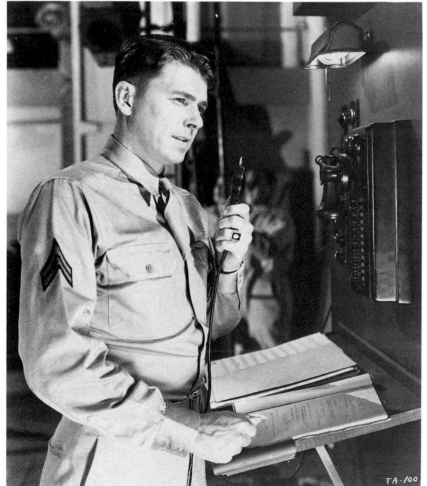

TA-100

Flynn had wanted the scene for himself, and it would certainly have stood him in better stead with the film's critics and its more responsible adult audiences than his line at the end. Flynn, flying his men safely back to England in a stolen bomber, was called upon to yell triumphantly 'Now for Australia and a crack at the Japs!' which caused a considerable stir at the time.

Reagan's next war film had him teamed up with 300 regular US servicemen in Irving Berlin's blockbuster musical *This Is the Army* (1943) directed by the highly experienced Michael Curtiz. Planned as a money-making as well as a morale-boosting, flag-waving contribution to America's war effort, the film was based on Berlin's enormously successful Broadway show and included among its 19 musical numbers such all-time favourites as 'God Bless America,' 'This Is the Army, Mr Jones,' and 'Oh, How I Hate to Get Up in the Morning.' As far as most of the cast, including Reagan, were concerned the film was a military assignment and the only money they received from being in it was their usual military pay. Film and stage production together contributed many millions of dollars to the Army Relief Fund.

Reagan's role in the film was that of Johnny Jones, author of the show in which the soldiers take part in the film. George Murphy was his father, and the show's producer, and the love interest was supplied by

Joan Leslie. The end of the film saw young Johnny Jones going off to war, just as his father had done in the First World War. The final performance of the show had taken place in Washington before the President, and Johnny had wed his sweetheart.

Reagan was seconded from the army to make the film, and was whisked straight back in to carry on making training films as soon as it was completed. The war had been over, and Reagan out of the army, for two years, when he was put back in uniform in 1947 for his next film with a war background. The war was very much in the background, and romance very much to the fore, however, for the film was *The Voice of the Turtle*, a sophisticated romantic comedy, based on the successful John Van Druten Broadway play.

Although additional characters were added for the film version, the story of *The Voice of the Turtle* remained that of two girls and a guy, who began in pursuit of one girl and ended in love with the other.

The guy, army sergeant Bill Page, played by Reagan, is on leave, all alone, and decides to visit New York to pursue an acquaintance with a delightful actress Olive Lashbrook (Eve Arden), but she, being otherwise en-gaged with a naval commander, allows him to be taken over, quite innocently of course, by another hopeful young actress, Sally Middleton, played by the attractive Eleanor Parker. Sally, between dates at the time and anyway rather short of boyfriends in war-time New York, offers Bill her apartment while he is in town.

It is not long before Bill has become very interested in Sally, and not too long before she is reciprocating his interest. Meanwhile, Olive, away from the navy, also notices Bill's masculine charms and endeavours to stop romance burgeoning between him and Sally. It's no go, of course, and eventually she has to concede good-humoured defeat, leaving Bill and Sally to find true love.

Not exactly an original tale, and the film was lightweight stuff for an actor who had been hoping for something much stronger in which to re-establish himself after the too-long gap since *King's Row* had marked him out for real stardom. But the script was good and Irving Rapper's sympathetic direction helped draw good performances from all three actors so that the film pleased its au-diences, and is remembered with affection by its male star.

Reagan was back in uniform for *The Voice of the Turtle* (Warner Bros.) although the war was by then over. It was a love story in which Reagan began by pursuing Eve Arden (left) but fell in love with newcomer Eleanor Parker (centre), who hides him behind the door.

Right: The marriage which causes the trouble in *John Loves Mary* (Warner Bros.) was contracted by Reagan to get his bride into the States for his pal, and her true love, Jack Carson. The proffered cigar seems poor reward for his glum predicament.

Below: Reagan in a spot of bother in the farce-like *John Loves Mary* (Warner Bros.) in which, as a sergeant returning from the war with a GI bride, he has difficulty explaining the situation to his fiancée Patricia Neal.

36

Reagan wore an army sergeant's stripes again for *John Loves Mary* (1949), though this time the sergeant was returning from the war, not just on leave. *John Loves Mary* was originally a Broadway play by Norman Krasna, and was very successful, audiences loving the farce-like complications of the plot. It was less successful as a film, though enjoyable enough to ensure that Warners did not lose their money.

The problem was partly, of course, that the story line was out-of-date: the war had been over four years, and most soldiers had long-since returned. The plot was pretty thin, too, depending as it did on the hero, John (Reagan, of course) being unable to explain at the outset to his fiancée, Mary (Patricia Neal, making her cinema debut after an acting career which had included playing in 'The Voice of the Turtle' on Broadway) just why he was returning from the war in Europe with a GI bride.

Well, yes, the bride was his, but he had only married her to enable her to get into the States to catch up with her real love Fred

(Jack Carson) who had once saved John's life, which was why John was doing them both this favour now. Unfortunately, back in the States Fred was already married to someone else and there was a baby on the way . . . Then the GI bride turned out to have been married before, to another GI whom she thought had been killed in action, but here he was turning up again like the proverbial bad penny . . . But perhaps it was not so bad after all because it meant that the GI bride and John could not really be married to each other, so John was free to love Mary. Phew.

Reagan's next venture into service life was something quite different, and much more satisfying. *The Hasty Heart* (1950) was once again based on a successful play, by John Patrick, and was a moving, heart-tugging tale set in a British army hospital in Burma during the Second World War. The story centred on the way in which one of the hospital's patients, a prickly, dour young Scots soldier called Lachie, had to come to terms with the discovery that he was dying and

The Hasty Heart (Warner Bros.) was a moving story of patients in a war-time hospital, in which Richard Todd scored a great success. He is seen offering a home in Scotland to American patient Reagan, watched by Ralph Michael, John Sherman, Howard Marion Crawford and Orlando Martins.

with the realization that his fellow patients were trying to offer him friendship not because they pitied him but because they cared about him as a person.

While *The Hasty Heart* was a triumph for Richard Todd, the relatively inexperienced British actor who played Lachie, it was also one of Ronald Reagan's most successful films. His role, that of Yank, the kind-hearted but strong-minded American whose compassion led him to break through the hard shell in which the solitary Lachie had encased himself, was a sympathetic one and Reagan handled it well. Patricia Neal was also in this film, playing the gentle and lovely ward sister.

By the time Reagan was again back in uniform on the screen, in *Prisoner of War* (1954) he was no longer under sole contract to Warner Brothers, and the good scripts did not seem to be coming in. When the script for this film came from Metro-Goldwyn-Mayer, the increasingly anti-Communist Reagan was immediately interested. Its theme, based on hard fact, was how captured American soldiers were ill-treated and brain-washed in prisoner-of-war camps in communist Korea. Reagan's part was that of an army officer, Web Sloane, who parachuted behind enemy lines to discover the truth of the dreadful stories that were filtering out of Korea.

The film was made at considerable speed, largely in order to catch current public interest in the subject, which was perhaps one reason why it made little impression, despite the presence in the cast of such good actors as Oscar Homolka (as a Russian officer) and Steve Forrest (as an American soldier defying his captors).

Reagan made another venture into similar territory at this time when he narrated the script for a controversial American documentary, *The Ultimate Weapon – Men's Minds*, whose thesis was that captured American soldiers often put up insufficient fight against the brain-washing influence of their Korean captors because their home up-bringing all too often lacked moral fibre.

Reagan's last service role, *Hellcats of the Navy* (1957), was also the last feature film he made for the cinema. By this time he was well established in television, a fact which may have cushioned the disappointment of his apparently early retirement from movie stardom – he was only in his mid-forties, after all. His wife, Nancy Davis, was also in *Hellcats* playing his fiancée, which may have made the project more enjoyable, but it was, in fact, a rather pedestrian farewell to a twenty-year career.

As with *Prisoner of War*, this film was based on fact, and concerned a Second World War operation in Japanese waters which Ad-

miral Chester Nimitz had commanded. The main problem was to get American submarines through the mine-infested waters of the Sea of Japan and the Tsushima Strait. Reagan played submarine Commander Casey Abbot whose mission it was to penetrate the minefields and return with some of the Japanese mines for US Navy experts to examine and try to establish why ordinary sonar equipment could not detect them.

Numerous encounters with the Japanese enemy, in one of which Abbot's submarine was destroyed, plus a sub-plot involving a hostile junior officer and the commander's girlfriend Helen (Nancy Davis) kept the story moving along briskly enough, but somehow the whole film seemed to be rather old hat: it should have been made about 12 years before, in the heat of real war.

Above: A poster for Reagan's last feature film, *Hellcats of the Navy* (Columbia), in which he got star billing, thereby managing to leave while at the top. His wife, Nancy Davis, was co-starred, and played his fiancée.

Far left: On the set of *Prisoner of War* (MGM), a film which interested Reagan because of its theme of American soldiers being brain-washed by Communists during the Korean War. Here he hams it up with Robert Horton and Dewey Martin.

RONALD REAGAN'S LADIES: AN INTERLUDE

One of the things the young Ronald Reagan thought he was going to enjoy most about his budding screen career was the chances it would give him to meet and, with a bit of luck, to kiss many of the pretty girls who made up a large proportion of Hollywood's population.

Being still young and impressionable, he naturally suffered from 'leadingladyitis', a disease which caused him to fall in love, if only temporarily, with every pretty young actress with whom he worked. It was not a debilitating disease, and did not curb his enthusiastic anticipation of his first screen kiss.

June Travis was the pretty girl, *Love Is on the Air* was the film, and the first kiss was a big disappointment, for Reagan was quickly to discover that screen kissing, like many other aspects of the cinema, is often a delusion. However deeply felt it may look, a screen kiss, Reagan discovered in the 1930s, should be only a chaste and very gentle pressing of the lips; anything more passionate, and the girl's face gets squashed out of shape, the feller's collar gets in a twist, his head gets in the way of the lights, and the illusion of romance is shattered.

This incident went no way towards blighting Reagan's screen relationships with women, and in the course of his 53 movies, he worked with a good number of Hollywood's more attractive women, though never with any from the really top flight. Because his own career was never glamorous, he was not to know the reflected glory of working with the really legendary women of 1940s and 1950s Hollywood, which was perhaps as well, for his own 'nice fellow' personality would probably have been completely swamped by the super-charged characters of a Garbo or a Dietrich. He acted in a film with Bette Davis and in another with the lovely Olivia de Havilland, but other men got the girl in both pictures. Not for Ronnie Reagan the chance to win on the screen such glittering prizes as Rita Hayworth and Betty Grable.

This, like other things about his career, was partly a result of being contracted to Warners, who at the time he worked for them, were not much into the glamorous, all-singing all-dancing all-colour kind of film for which the studio would have needed a bigger supply of really glamorous women than they had. Even so, while no one apart from his two wives ever seems to have made a place for herself in his private life, some very charming ladies found their way into Ronald Reagan's screen life. Foremost among them was Warner Brothers' 'Oomph Girl', Ann Sheridan.

'Oomph? What's oomph?' brilliant Hollywood photographer George Hurrell is supposed to have asked when called upon to

The young Reagan, embarking on a screen career, was naturally aware that one of the benefits would be mixing with some of the world's most beautiful women, although the title of his 1947 film, *Stallion Road*, is not meant to suggest anything. A delectable co-star of that movie was Alexis Smith.

Below: Another starring role with Ann Sheridan was in *Juke Girl* (Warner Bros.), their third film together, and not worthy of their acting skills.

photograph Sheridan displaying this desirable though nebulous quality. Indeed, no-one knew what it was, unless it was something like 'It', which you either had or you had not; it had just been a successful publicity wheeze that had saddled Sheridan with the title. She was, in fact, much more than just a very pretty and sexy looking girl who could put across a song in a rich, golden voice, for she also had a strong character that allowed her to stand out even when teamed opposite other strong characters like James Cagney, Humphrey Bogart or George Raft.

Sheridan and Reagan worked together on five films, in three of which – *Angels Wash Their Faces*, *King's Row* and *Juke Girl* – they were the leads, though only *King's Row* was worthy of the talents of either of them. In it, Sheridan played the out-going, slightly tomboyish and warm-hearted Randy, the working-class girl who eventually won the heart of Drake McHugh, her devoted care helping him to come to terms with the loss of his legs.

Another girl to find a place on several cast lists with Reagan was his first wife, Jane Wyman. They began dating while playing in what was to be their best film together, *Brother Rat*. This was in the early 1940s, when Warners had Wyman type-cast as a large-eyed, blonde, pert little lady, fine for light comedies.

Warners kept her mainly in programmers and B features, with the occasional A, like *Brother Rat*, and she had to go to other

Far left: A glamour portrait of
Ann Sheridan, who like Clara
Bow, the 'It' girl, was also
given a sexy soubriquet, the
'Oomph' girl.

Left: Jane Wyman, Reagan's
first wife, acted with him in
many films. Although her
greatest success came in an
Oscar-winning, difficult
actress's role in *Johnny
Belinda*, in her early days she
posed for the obligatory clean-
cut pin-up pictures.

Right: Laraine Day played opposite Reagan in *The Bad Man* in 1941. Her roles never quite matched her acting ability.

Above: Priscilla Lane was one of Reagan's earliest leading ladies, and acted with him in the 1930s. This is a publicity shot for the Reagan movie *Million Dollar Baby* (Warner Bros.).

happened to her or being able to tell anyone else.

It was at this time she divorced Reagan, leading him to make the bitter and oft-quoted remark that Johnny Belinda was the only co-respondent he could have cited in his divorce case. She claimed that one of the problems had been the Screen Actors Guild, which kept Reagan busy, and perhaps he had indeed been less supporting than he might have been at a time when she was feeling the stress of a difficult role.

While Jane Wyman went her way completely separately from Reagan, building up a film and television career that was longer and more successful than his (and also marrying again in 1952, the year in which he married Nancy Davis, though her new marriage lasted only two years), it is probably true to say that without him in her past, she would not have made a successful come-back in the 1980s as the star of a television soap opera.

During the 1940s, when Reagan's screen career seemed as if it might be a successful one, the young actresses with whom he worked were more often than not charming and intelligent as well as possessing the obligatory above-average good looks. Laraine Day, Priscilla Lane (the most successful of five actress sisters, three of whom made careers for themselves in Hollywood), Patricia Neal and Eleanor Parker all added style to the movies in which they played opposite Reagan. Apart from Patricia Neal, they were none of them to go on to make outstanding careers for themselves in the cinema. Reagan himself had not even wanted the talented, red-haired Eleanor Parker to have the role Warners gave her in *The Voice of the Turtle*, thinking that someone like June Allyson might give a better boost to his post-war career. He had the grace to admit he had been wrong: Eleanor Parker turned out to be good, and it seems a pity now that she quite quickly dwindled into supporting roles.

Patricia Neal, who played with Reagan in two films, had as much style and ability as Parker, but she also possessed a certain extra something, an inner warmth and humour, which, though it failed to surface in the indifferent *John Loves Mary*, lit up her role in *The Hasty Heart*. In this film, which was also one of Reagan's best, she was good, making a memorable part out of the role of the nurse over-seeing a ward of soldiers in a Burma field hospital, and serving notice that here was a young actress who might be going places. Which she was, most notably in *Breakfast at Tiffany's* (1961) and in *Hud* (1963), in which her performance, playing opposite an equally good Paul Newman,

studios to prove that she could do better. She stopped letting the studio bleach her hair and found herself parts that were more than light comedies, which was the only kind of film she was ever to make with her second husband, Reagan. She reached the peak of her career with *Johnny Belinda* in 1948. Her Oscar-winning performance in this film had been difficult, harrowing work, for she played a deaf mute who was raped and made pregnant, without understanding what had

won her both a Hollywood Best Actress Oscar and a British Academy Best Actress award.

Once Reagan's career had passed its peak, actresses of this calibre no longer seemed to be around to offer support. Doris Day turned up a couple of times, most notably in the successful *The Winning Team* (1952) where her playing of the wife sticking by her husband through thick and thin was sincere rather than scintillating, and the promising and beautiful Swedish actress, Viveca Lindfors, made one film with Reagan, *Night unto Night* (1949), which was too melodramatic to make it at the box office.

What Reagan's producers chose to offer him instead of real ability was sex-appeal, twice in the shape of curvaceous blonde Virginia Mayo and three times in the form of the red-headed Rhonda Fleming. Of the two, Virginia Mayo added the most spice to Reagan's post-war films, particularly in *The Girl from Jones Beach* (1949), in which box-office hit she looked stunning when let loose in a white bathing suit, and in *She's Working Her Way Through College* which was less successful but still amusing.

Above: In *Storm Warning* (Warner Bros.) Reagan had two charming actresses on set with him, Doris Day and Ginger Rogers.

Right: Reagan with the beautiful Swedish actress Viveca Lindfors in *Night unto Night* (Warner Bros.). She always looked good in costume swashbucklers, but her film with Reagan was disappointing.

Far right: Rhonda Fleming provided the eye-appeal in some of Reagan's films in the early 1950s, none of which did much for either of their careers.

48

TIME FOR CHANGE

Far right, top: A showcard for Reagan's first post-war film *Stallion Road* (Warner Bros.), which should have starred him with Humphrey Bogart and Lauren Bacall, but they dropped out.

Far right, bottom: Shirley Temple, the child star of the 1930s, was attempting the transition into romantic roles in 1947, and in *That Hagen Girl* (Warner Bros.) the much older Reagan had to woo and win her.

Below: Reagan as a vet in *Stallion Road* (Warner Bros.), sharing a toast in the great outdoors with Alexis Smith.

When Captain Ronald Reagan was discharged from the US army in 1945 he went back to Warner Brothers, where the returning soldier was given the makings of a distinctly comfortable future in the form of a new exclusive, seven-year, one-million-dollar contract. On the whole, taking one thing with another, life was to deal kindly with him in the coming years. True, his wife Jane Wyman would divorce him in 1948, but it would not be long before he would meet the girl who was to be his second wife, Nancy Davis. He was also to become deeply involved in the workings of the actors union, the Screen Actors Guild. This union involvement, rekindling an interest in politics which had lain dormant since his college days, was eventually to take him out of films altogether and into a full-time political career.

The one aspect of his life which did not look too rosy a few years after the war, was his film career. Far from being able to build on the personal success of *King's Row*, Reagan seemed all too often to be back in the position of B movie action man. He had a few good parts, notably in *The Hasty Heart* (1950) and *The Winning Team* (1952), but there was an awful lot of second-rate stuff, too, and by the middle 1950s it was clear that the skids were under the movie career of Ronald Reagan: only one film starring him was released in 1954, and that came after a 14-month gap. It was about this time that Reagan began making the switch from the cinema to television, which would supply his income until full-time politics called him in the form of the governorship of California in 1966.

RONALD REAGAN
ALEXIS SMITH
ZACHARY SCOTT

STALLION ROAD

WARNER PICTURE

DIRECTED BY
JAMES V. KERN

47/173

Reagan's first post-war film, *Stallion Road* (1947), might have got him off to a really grand start if Humphrey Bogart, due to take part as well, had not dropped out, being replaced by the less effective Zachary Scott. Lauren Bacall should have been in it, too, but she decided to follow her husband's lead and not take part; Alexis Smith got her role.

Even without the Bogarts, *Stallion Road* was not a bad movie, and Reagan gave an effective performance, at the same time thoroughly enjoying the chance the film gave him to work with horses. He did his own riding and jumping sequences in the film, in which he was cast as veterinary surgeon Larry Hanrahan battling to control a killer outbreak of anthrax among local cattle.

Reagan's next film is probably best forgotten. It was *That Hagen Girl*, intended as a vehicle to help child-star Shirley Temple make the difficult transition to adult movies. Reagan was nearer 40 than 30, Shirley was 19, and the script called for him to fall in love with her, propose marriage and be accepted. Reagan was sure picture-goers would hate this and begged Warners to keep him out of it. They insisted and the film was done as scripted, but hostile reaction at a sneak-preview led to a hasty re-write of the end which only managed to leave audiences in some mystification as to just what Shirley and Ronald were doing going off on a train together.

There were no doubts about what was going on in *Night unto Night* (1949); unfortunately, the whole story was too unbelievably melodramatic to carry much conviction. Reagan's role was that of a biochemist suffering from incurable and worsening epilepsy, who rents a secluded Florida beach house where he hopes to be able to carry on his work peacefully. The lady from whom he rents the house, played by Viveca Lindfors, has problems of her own, believing that she can hear the voice of her dead husband every time she enters the house. The fact that the husband's body, with 4000 miles of American coast to choose from, gets washed ashore on the beach below the house, is too much for any audience, however credulous, to swallow. In fact, there was not a lot the cast, which included Broderick Crawford, could do with this one.

After this, the light and funny *The Girl from Jones Beach* could only be a distinct improvement. In this picture, Reagan had some lively comedy scenes as a pin-up artist with a style not a million miles from that of the world-famous Vargas of *Playboy* magazine. As the artist's name is Bob Randolph, the ideal girl he depicts is known as 'the Randolph Girl'. Shapely Virginia Mayo, supplying the female glamour, appears as a serious-minded school teacher who just happens to be relaxing in an eye-stunning bathing costume on Jones Beach when a television company PR man (Eddie Bracken) and Randolph come along in search of a real 'Randolph Girl' to boost one of the TV company's programmes. Randolph's pursuit of the reluctant bathing-beauty teacher takes him into her citizenship class, disguised as a Czech, which allowed Reagan to play about with funny accents.

After a guest appearance as a barbershop customer in *It's a Great Feeling*, a zany Jack Carson comedy in which Warners had a sizable part of their list of contract players making brief appearances (Errol Flynn was Doris Day's smalltown boyfriend, Jeffrey Bushdinkle), Reagan did *The Hasty Heart* in England, his first trip outside the United States, then came back to star in a movie for Universal, *Louisa* (1950), having persuaded Warners to release him from his exclusive contract with them.

Viveca Lindfors was a glamorous widow who became Reagan's landlady in *Night unto Night* (Warner Bros.), an improbable melodrama.

The Girl from Jones Beach
(Warner Bros.) was shapely
Virginia Mayo, and she and
Reagan used the beach to
advantage for games of
leapfrog between shots.

Right: *Louisa* (Universal) was a pleasant comedy involving three generations. Piper Laurie was the teenaged daughter of Reagan, and Charles Coburn was one of the suitors of Reagan's mother.

Below: Reagan switched from comedy to a Klu Klux Klan murder story for *Storm Warning* (Warner Bros.), in which he appeared with Doris Day, Ginger Rogers and Steve Cochran.

Louisa was another comedy, and an enjoyable one, though this time Reagan had moved out of romantic lead status into that of middle-aged dependable in a domestic situation.

A happily married architect with a daughter, Hal Norton (Reagan) also has a mother, the lively and flighty Louisa of the film's title (Spring Byington). The romantic complications of widowed Louisa's life, which involve her with two suitors (Edmund Gwenn and Charles Coburn), and their effect on the harassed Hal, give the film its basic plot, with the unravelling of the complications making for an amusing and enjoyable movie.

After this pleasant interlude at Universal, made all the more agreeable because he was working with – for him – such new faces as Spring Byington, Edmund Gwenn, Ruth Hussey (as his wife) and Piper Laurie (as his teenage daughter), Reagan went back to Warners for his first film under the new contract he had worked out with them, which called for him to make one picture a year for three years and allowed him to freelance with other studios.

The contrast between *Louisa* and this new film, *Storm Warning* (1951) could hardly have been more marked. With *Storm Warning* Warners were doing their social-consciousness bit, and it was a grim anti-Klu Klux Klan piece.

Ginger Rogers starred as Marsha Mitchell, a New York fashion model discovering that her younger sister Lucy (Doris Day) is married to a member of the Klu Klux Klan whom Marsha has just witnessed committing a brutal murder. Subpoenaed by local District Attorney Burt Rainey (Reagan) to tell all she had seen of the murder, Marsha, begged by Lucy to say nothing, denies having seen who committed the crime.

This sisterly action does not save Marsha from a beating at the hands of her brutal brother-in-law, who also attacks his pregnant wife. There follows another scene of threatened violence at a meeting of the Klan, at which Marsha is saved from another beating only by the timely arrival of the District Attorney, intent on pursuing and breaking up the Klan. Eventually he succeeds in this, but only after a shooting in which Lucy is wounded by her husband, who is himself gunned down by the police.

It was a violent and unpleasant story, but also one with a serious purpose, convincingly acted by the cast, including Reagan.

From this, it was back to Universal for the film which has caused President Reagan more retrospective embarrassment than any other he made: *Bedtime for Bonzo*.

Bonzo was a chimpanzee, and an animal of considerable intelligence and natural charm who is, so we are told, currently a campus movie club favourite across America. Which is not surprising. It is not every day that a President of the United States has to admit to having taken second place to an ape.

Not that Reagan ever allows any embarrassment he might feel to show. On the contrary, he insists that *Bedtime for Bonzo* was a good film, on a basically important theme.

The co-star who has caused most comment since Reagan became President is a chimpanzee. Here they are together in *Bedtime for Bonzo* (Universal).

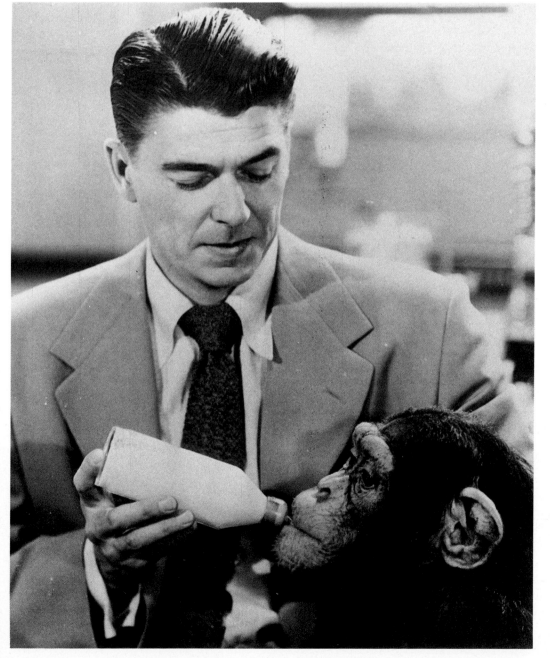

After all, the film-makers were only doing what serious researchers were also doing in universities at the same time: investigating the role of heredity versus environment in the development of character. Be that as it may, Bonzo stole the show from Reagan's professor of psychology and from everyone else in the film, including Walter Slezak as the zoology professor from whom Reagan borrowed his chimp and Diana Lynn as the nurse hired to become a surrogate mother to Bonzo.

Reagan moved on to Paramount for his next film, *The Last Outpost*, an entertaining Western set in the Arizona desert at the time of the Civil War. It was the first time that Reagan, despite his skill as a rider and his interest in the history of the American West, had been given a part in a real Western, and he enjoyed making it.

The sort of Western that pleases the kids rather than makes the buffs and critics hand out superlatives, *The Last Outpost* was put together by the experienced Paramount production team of Pine and Thomas. Their story was based on the true fact of the Civil War that the Confederates had more than

once tried to intercept gold shipments from the south-west meant for the Union forces. The film threw in Indian trouble in the form of an Apache rising in Arizona caused when a white man shot an Apache chief, and family conflict in the form of two brothers who found themselves on opposite sides in the Civil War. Reagan was Confederate cavalry officer Vance Britten sent to Arizona to try to halt and re-route the gold shipment, and Bruce Bennet was his brother, Jeb, a cavalry officer on the Union side whom fate had decreed should be the man charged with seeing the gold safely through to its destination.

The romance was supplied by gorgeous redhead Rhonda Fleming as Vance Britten's former fiancée, now married to someone else, and there was plenty of action, with pounding hooves, whizzing bullets and whooping Indians. Reagan, handsome and dashing in cavalry uniform, looked good on horseback. No doubt his fan mail increased as a result.

Hong Kong (1952), another Paramount picture, may not have done so much for his fan mail because he was working with an-

Reagan, Noah Beery Jr, and Bill Williams in *The Last Output* (Paramount), in which Reagan was a Confederate cavalry officer attempting to steal a gold shipment *en route* for the Union forces.

Color by
CHNICOLOR

THE
**LAST
OUTPOST**

starring

RONALD REAGAN **RHONDA FLEMING** with BRUCE BENNETT · BILL WILLIAMS directed by LEWIS R. FOSTER Written for the Screen by Geoffrey Homes · George Worthing Yates & Winston Miller
NOAH BEERY · PETER HANSON produced by WILLIAM H. PINE & WILLIAM C. THOMAS **A PARAMOUNT PICTURE**

other scene-stealer, a four-year-old Chinese boy, Danny Chang, who not only looked exceedingly cute, but was a better actor than Bonzo.

Another Pine-Thomas adventure yarn, this was an Eastern, rather than a Western, being set in what the film's publicity dubbed 'the port of a thousand dangers'. Reagan was Jeff Williams, an ex-serviceman down on his luck in post-war Hong Kong, trying to scratch a living out of selling army surplus.

Caught up in an affray on mainland China, Jeff finds himself burdened with a solitary little Chinese boy as he makes his escape. Helped by an American Red Cross Worker, Victoria (Rhonda Fleming), Jeff and Wei Lin, the little boy, make it back to Hong Kong. After a series of adventures with a representative selection of the city's vast hordes of bad men, during the course of which Wei Lin gets kidnapped, Jeff and Victoria marry and settle down to a life of domestic bliss, planning to spend their Sundays visiting Wei Lin in the local orphanage.

It all played a bit like a strip cartoon story, but Reagan acted as if he believed in it all, giving *Hong Kong* a certain credibility. By this time a convinced anti-Communist, Reagan probably did see the film as a good piece of anti-Red propaganda.

He went back to the Warners lot for his next two films, the light and fluffy musical comedy, *She's Working Her Way through College*, and the biopic, *The Winning Team*.

In the musical, which was quite a pleasant example of the genre, though not the sort that gets mentioned in histories of film musicals, Virginia Mayo was the dancing star, Angela Gardner, who was working her way through college, and Reagan was the quiet, respectably married professor in whose house Angela obtained board and lodging. There was plenty of scope for Virginia Mayo to display her dancing talents because Angela was able to persuade the professor that he should abandon his usual practice of producing a serious play for the college's annual drama event and put on a musical instead.

A showcard for *The Last Outpost* (Paramount), Reagan's first part in a full-blooded Western, in which he was able to use his skill with horses.

59

Above: In *Hong Kong*
(Paramount), Reagan and co-
star Rhonda Fleming had to
contend not only with 'the
port of a thousand dangers'
but also with the risk of being
overshadowed by a Chinese
child actor, Danny Chang.

Right: *She's Working Her
Way Through College* (Warner
Bros.) and this is how she was
doing it. Virginia Mayo again,
as a dancer persuading her
professor, Reagan, who seems
to be finding her legs
somewhat distracting, to put
on a musical.

Music was by Sammy Cahn and Vernon
Duke, colour was by Technicolor, and the
whole thing made a pleasing evening's entertainment for cinema audiences.

The Winning Team was a much more
serious affair, being a slice-of-life drama
based on the true story of baseball pitcher
Grover Cleveland Alexander, a pre-First
World War baseball star (played by Reagan)
who made the game's history books by coming back from the depths of illness (epilepsy,
in fact, though Warners preferred not to say
so), alcoholism, the minor leagues and even
a circus sideshow into the big time of World
Series baseball in the 1920s.

The part suited Reagan to a 'T', he enjoyed
the weeks of filming and hours of baseball
practice and turned in a sincerely felt performance that aroused considerable admiration, especially among baseball fans.

The film was a love story, too, giving
Doris Day a chance to make a good impression in the part of Alexander's wife, Aimee,
who stuck by him through thick and thin
and finally managed to persuade ace baseball

Reagan enjoyed his role in *The Winning Team* (Warner Bros.) and he produced a convincing performance as the famous baseball pitcher Grover Cleveland Alexander, who defeated illness to star in the World Series.

manager, Rogers Hornsby (Frank Lovejoy) to give her husband another chance at the top. As the lobby cards put it, here were 'two people who won something far bigger than a World Series baseball game'.

The Winning Team marked the end of Reagan's partnership – if that is the right word – with Warners, his arguing with Jack Warner over parts having become more than either could live with, and Reagan moved out into the cold, hard world of Hollywood, where the good scripts were getting harder to find. Jack Warner must have smiled a wry smile or two in 1973 when one of the chief speakers at his testimonial dinner was the Governor of California, Ronald 'the Gipper' Reagan.

The Winning Team was also to be the last film with any pretensions to real worth that Reagan was to make. His next film, *Tropic Zone* (1953), made for Paramount, has been dismissed by its star as 'a sand-and-bananas'

61

Above: Relaxing for a studio publicity shot during the making of *Tropic Zone* (Paramount) are the stars of the picture, Rhonda Fleming, Reagan, Estelita and Noah Beery Jr.

Right: While marshal Reagan and his men collect guns in their efforts to clean up Cottonwood in *Law and Order* (Universal), Dorothy Malone turns up to tell him she is prepared to marry him.

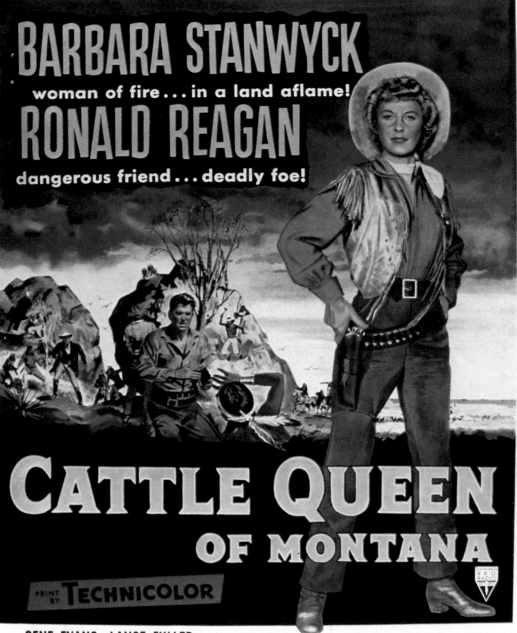

REGISTERED No. F 20366

BARBARA STANWYCK
woman of fire...in a land aflame!
RONALD REAGAN
dangerous friend...deadly foe!

CATTLE QUEEN OF MONTANA

PRINT BY **TECHNICOLOR**

with GENE EVANS · LANCE FULLER · Directed by ALLAN DWAN · Screenplay by ROBERT BLEES & HOWARD ESTABROOK · Produced by BENEDICT BOGEAUS

Reagan was an undercover army officer in *Cattle Queen of Montana* (RKO) investigating cattle rustling. It enabled him to play a Western hero again, a role which he played more often in his last films than in his earlier ones.

epic, which is a fair enough summary of a dreary programmer about the corruption and nastiness involved in growing bananas in Central America.

Law and Order, made for Universal, was slightly better: it was merely unmemorable. Reagan took the role because he liked the idea of making Westerns, and Warners had never given him the opportunity to do so. This one had him as a lawman who, having cleaned up Tombstone, Arizona, wants to take early retirement and become a cattle rancher. Instead events decree that he must

clean up another frontier town first, in the course of which he has to arrest his own brother for a killing, thus demonstrating to all that the law is the law and must be obeyed.

A whole year went by before Reagan next saw a film script he wanted to do, *Prisoner of War* (1954). The following year, he put on Western garb again to play in RKO's *Cattle Queen of Montana*. The Queen was Sierra Nevada Jones (Barbara Stanwyck) fighting the baddies trying to destroy her ranch. Reagan was Farrell, an undercover

army officer in the region to investigate reports of cattle rustling and Indian disturbances. The budget on this one was low, and it showed.

Tennessee's Partner had Reagan once more in the saddle with a gun in his hand. Based extremely loosely on a story by Bret Harte, *Tennessee's Partner* was set in a Gold Rush era mining town where Tennessee (John Payne) made a more than reasonable living off the gambling table pickings in a saloon run by Rhonda Fleming. He was twice saved from being shot by Cowpoke (Reagan) and the two became buddies of a sort, though there was trouble between them over a girl. In the end, Cowpoke got himself killed in a shoot-out; the funeral was grand, but the film wasn't.

Apart from *Hellcats of the Navy*, made in 1957, this was Reagan's last real picture show – so far: commentators say there could still be rich pickings for a former movie star who has been President of the United States. Reagan made *The Killers*, freely adapted from Ernest Hemingway's short story, for television in 1964, but it looked too nasty to the television moguls and it got dumped into second-string movie houses. And that, as far

BENEDICT BOGEAUS presents

JOHN PAYNE
RONALD REAGAN
RHONDA FLEMING
COLEEN GRAY

in *Bret Harte's*
Tennessee's Partner

Print by **TECHNICOLOR**   **SUPERSCOPE**

TONY CARUSO · MORRIS ANKRUM   Directed by ALLAN DWAN · Screenplay by MILTON KRIMS, D.D. BEAUCHAMP and GRAHAM BAKER & TEDDI SHERMAN · Produced by BENEDICT BOGEAUS

Above: Tennessee in *Tennessee's Partner* (RKO) was John Payne (right), who made his living in the gambling saloon run by Rhonda Fleming. Tennessee's partner was Reagan (left).

Left: Reagan's last film, *The Killers* (NBC-TV), was based on an Ernest Hemingway story and in it he had a new leading lady, Angie Dickinson (right). The film was actually made for television, but was released in the cinema.

Far left, top: Barbara Stanwyck was one of Reagan's many leading ladies. She had the title role in *Cattle Queen of Montana* (RKO), rejoicing under the name of Sierra Nevada Jones and defending her ranch against baddies.

Far left, bottom: Reagan was a cowboy again in *Tennessee's Partner* (RKO), this time getting himself killed before the fade-out. Rhonda Fleming was with him once again in a film about the Gold Rush.

66

as the screen career of Ronald Reagan, film star, was concerned, was that.

He was not the only actor to receive notice to quit in the 1950s. Competition from television and nose-diving box-office takings caused all the Hollywood studios to part with large numbers of contract players, many of them big names, who had been stalwarts of hundreds of movies for ten or twenty years. Some turned to nightclubs, legitimate theatre, summer stock or road shows; others disappeared without trace. Many of the lucky ones, including Ronald Reagan, made it to safe havens in television.

In fact, Ronald Reagan had found his feet in the world of television by the time *Cattle Queen of Montana* was released. He had already appeared in a number of television drama programmes before accepting an offer to become host of the 'General Electric Theater', a weekly drama series, in 1954. This proved to be a successful series, running for many years, in which Reagan sometimes took acting roles. One of these, in which his

wife, Nancy, and a turkey also had parts, was called 'A Turkey for the President'.

As part of his deal with General Electric, Reagan undertook to work in a public relations capacity for the company, visiting their plants all over the country and talking to employees about company policy and the relationship between business, the community and the country as a whole. It was perfect experience for the budding, increasingly conservative, politician which Reagan was at this time. He had had his first period as president of the Screen Actors Guild in the early 1950s, and was to have a second term in 1959, by which time, according to the political science specialists, some people were beginning to wonder if there might not be a whole lot more potential in Ronald Reagan than had been apparent so far.

He himself says he was happy with life as it was then, and a career in politics was far from his thoughts. He enjoyed working in television, and would host and act in a second popular series, 'Death Valley Days', be-

Above: Nelle Reagan, Ronald's mother, influenced his acting career and actually appeared in a film herself, *Strange Paradise*, made in 1952, in which she was a busybody aboard a luxury liner. In this picture Ronald and wife Nancy are helping Nelle Reagan plug the film on radio.

Far left: Reagan made a career in television in the 1950s and 1960s, and hosted a series called 'Death Valley Days' in which he also acted as a cowboy hero.

fore politics claimed him completely in the mid-1960s. He was also happily married again, to a former Broadway actress and movie starlet, Nancy Davis.

He had met Nancy in the course of his union duties with the Screen Actors Guild. Somebody somewhere thought that union member Nancy was a Communist supporter and kept sending her left-wing publications and putting her name on left-wing lists, all of which was naturally upsetting for a good girl who had never been left of centre in her life, or anywhere near it. Reagan, as president of her union, was called in to sort out the problem, which turned out to be one of

mistaken identity – there was another actress Nancy Davis who did have left-wing sympathies – and, in the process, ended up sorting out his own post-divorce loneliness at the same time. They were married in 1952 and have been the ideal couple ever since.

Reagan and Nancy made only one film together, *Hellcats of the Navy*, before Nancy decided that marriage and motherhood were more important than a career and stopped acting, except for the occasional television appearance.

If movie star careers were over for both of them, even more memorable roles were just round the corner.

The National Father's Day Committee announced Ronald Reagan as Screen Father of the Year in 1957, when he was pictured with wife Nancy and their three-year-old daughter, Patti.

RONALD REAGAN'S GREATEST ROLE

Ronald and Nancy Reagan have frequently said that their role as parents and family people has been the most important in their lives. Indeed, Ronald Reagan played his domestic role so effectively in the 1950s that he was voted Screen Father of the Year by the National Father's Day Committee of America in 1957. By this time they had a daughter, three-year-old Patti, and their son, Ron, would arrive to complete the family the following year.

It might, however, be truer to say of Ronald Reagan that his role as family man has been important to him as the stable foundation of his life, but that he would have been a very unhappy man indeed without his other careers in movies, politics and – we should not forget – ranching and horse breeding. Nor is it easy to judge just how much less interested Reagan would have been in the politics of the Screen Actors Guild if his movie career had really taken off. He was certainly proud enough of his performance in *King's Row* to screen the film over and over again for friends. Indeed, Jane Wyman has been quoted as saying that one of the reasons she left Reagan was that she just could not stand to watch 'that damn *King's Row*' one more time.

On the other hand, Wyman also made it clear that the main reason why their marriage failed was because she was bored and lonely in a relationship in which the Screen Actors Guild seemed to be playing a bigger part than herself, which suggests that it was pretty important to Reagan.

Reagan has always been a strong family man. Here he is with his family on the New York ferry, with, appropriately, the Statue of Liberty in the background.

Far left: As Governor of California in 1968, Ronald Reagan makes a 'V for Victory' sign during a 'Citizens for Reagan' rally at the Deauville Hotel, Miami, Florida.

Left: Nancy Reagan has always supported her husband in his political career. This event, while he was Governor of California, must have seemed like an old stars' reunion as they shared the spotlight with Charlton Heston and James Cagney.

In contrast to Wyman, Nancy Reagan has always been completely absorbed in her husband's political career. She once asked Reagan to cancel their subscription to a newspaper, the *Sacramento Bee*, in which an anti-Governor Reagan editorial had so incensed her that she refused to have the paper in the house. Reagan had delivery switched to his office so that he could continue to read the newspaper and keep Nancy happy at the same time.

In his autobiography, Reagan wrote at length about his work for the Screen Actors Guild, which is hardly surprising since the book was published in 1965, perhaps as part of a public relations build-up to his first campaign for the Governorship of California, and he would want to emphasize his political background. Be that as it may, the Screen Actors Guild, which he had joined early in his screen career, loomed large in the book. He also wrote, with a certain disarming naiveté, about his part in Hollywood's anti-Red investigations of the late 1940s. He was outspokenly anti-Communist, though he seems to have lacked the fanaticism which marked

best hope of wresting the USA's largest state from the Democrats. They were right.

Opponents and press ever since have tended to sneer at Reagan's Hollywood background, calling him a B-movie actor whose only knowledge of politics is how to act the role of politician. While this is demonstrably not so, there is no denying that Reagan's experience as a film actor has been an enormous asset to him as a politician. It is not just that his career and life have been spent completely outside the party system, so that he can appeal directly to voters, his image uncluttered in their minds by thoughts of what other politicians of his party may have said or done. It is also a matter of how he presents himself.

He was always an effective speaker before crowds, as witness the success of his speech-making to the students of Eureka College during their strike against the college administration in his freshman year, and he was good in more intimate debates between union and management, which is one reason why the Screen Actors Guild elected him their president six times.

His acting experience, which included stage, screen and radio, plus all that public speaking to General Electric employees across the nation, helped hone this basic talent into a very effective medium indeed. He knew how to use cameras and a microphone, how to pitch his voice for the best effect, and he was a good impromptu speaker.

He is, in fact, brilliant at using television and extremely skilled at presenting a positive image – and not just in set speeches, as on the famous occasion in 1964. He can present a good image in unrehearsed debate, too. Witness, for example, presidential candidate Reagan rebutting a charge from a distinctly over-excited Carter that, if elected, Reagan would 'divide North from South, Christian from Jew, and rural from urban'. Television news showed a clip of this excessive rhetoric, then switched to Reagan, playing the sage statesman, shaking his head more in sorrow than in anger and saying gently, sadly: 'He's reaching a point of hysteria that's hard to understand.' Round to Reagan.

Ronald Reagan himself has never tried to play down his past career, always giving the impression that he considers it a matter of which one should be proud, rather than ashamed. On more than one occasion he has used his Hollywood background and his own very real sense of humour to lighten a difficult occasion.

There was his first swearing-in as Governor of California in 1966, for instance. For

Far left: Reagan speaking during the Republican campaign for the Presidency, supported by all the razzmatazz of stars and stripes and candidates' boards.

Overleaf: The President and the First Lady perhaps thinking back to their Hollywood days as they pose with one of the descendants of the best friends who helped him sort out the fictional problems of the West.

Below: The President and Mrs Reagan relaxing at the White House. It was a long way to have come for a B movie actor with an interest in trade union activities.

Right: A picture taken seconds before the assassination attempt on the President. It shows all four people who were shot, Press Secretary James Brady (third from left), President Reagan, Policeman Thomas Delahanty (nearest the umbrella, and behind whom the gunman was hidden) and Secret Service agent Timothy McCarthy (right).

Far right: His greatest role. Ronald Wilson Reagan, President of the United States of America.

Below: President Reagan recovering after the attempt on his life, during a visit by Mrs Reagan. He told her he 'forgot to duck'.

political reasons, the swearing-in was held just after midnight. A large crowd assembled in the capitol rotunda at Sacramento, plus the media in full cry, gave a tense atmosphere to the occasion. Senator George Murphy, who had once played Reagan's father in *This Is the Army* and who was also a past president of the Screen Actors Guild, made the opening speech, there were other, carefully prepared and rather dull speeches, then it was the turn of the Governor-elect. There was a portentous hush – apart from the grinding of the television cameras – then Reagan turned to Senator Murphy and said 'Well, Murph, here we are on the late, late show again.' Everyone laughed, the tension disappeared, and the occasion became a warm friendly one.

Even the attempted assassination of President Reagan outside the Washington Hilton on 30 March 1980 did not find the actor in him wanting. 'Sorry, hon, I forgot to duck, but I'll make it,' he gallantly remarked to Nancy as they wheeled him off to the operating theatre. Later still, when asked how he was feeling, he reached back into his Hollywood past to use one of W. C. Fields' more memorable lines: 'Frankly, I'd rather be in Philadelphia.'

Only time will tell whether Ronald Reagan, the United States' 40th president, will be numbered among the great ones; in the meantime, Ronald Reagan will be doing his best to ensure that everything looks good. Even his worst critics usually said of him that his performances were always competent.

FILMOGRAPHY

Love Is on the Air. 1937. Warner Bros./First National. Director: Nick Grinde. With Eddie Acuff, Robert Barrat, June Travis.

Hollywood Hotel. 1937. Warner Bros./First National. Director: Busby Berkeley. With Dick Powell, Rosemary Lane, Lola Lane.

Swing Your Lady. 1938. Warner Bros. Director: Ray Enright. With Humphrey Bogart, Frank McHugh, Louise Fazenda.

Sergeant Murphy. 1938. Warner Bros. Director: B. Reeves Eason. With Mary Maguire, Donald Crisp.

Accidents Will Happen. 1938. Warner Bros. Director: William Clemens. With Gloria Blondell, Dick Purcell.

Cowboy from Brooklyn. (GB: *Romance and Rhythm*) 1938. Warner Bros. Director: Lloyd Bacon. With Dick Powell, Pat O'Brien, Priscilla Lane.

Boy Meets Girl. 1938. Warner Bros. Director: Lloyd Bacon. With James Cagney, Pat O'Brien.

Girls on Probation. 1938. Warner Bros. Director: William McGann. With Jane Bryan, Anthony Averill, Sheila Bromley.

Brother Rat. 1938. Warner Bros. Director: William Keighley. With Wayne Morris, Priscilla Lane, Eddie Albert, Jane Wyman.

Going Places. 1939. Warner Bros./Cosmopolitan. Director: Ray Enright. With Dick Powell, Anita Louise, Allen Jenkins.

Secret Service of the Air. 1939. Warner Bros. Director: Noel Smith. With John Litel, James Stephenson, Eddie Foy Jr.

Dark Victory. 1939. Warner Bros./First National. Director: Edmund Goulding. With Bette Davis, George Brent, Humphrey Bogart.

Code of the Secret Service. 1939. Warner Bros. Director: Noel Smith. With Rosella Towne, Eddie Foy Jr.

Naughty but Nice. 1939. Warner Bros. Director: Ray Enright. With Dick Powell, Gale Page, Ann Sheridan.

Hell's Kitchen. 1939. Warner Bros. Directors: Lewis Seiler, E. A. Dupont. With Grant Mitchell, Stanley Fields, Margaret Lindsay, the Dead End Kids.

Angels Wash their Faces. 1939. Warner Bros. Director: Ray Enright. With Ann Sheridan, the Dead End Kids.

Smashing the Money Ring. 1939. Warner Bros. Director: Terry Morse. With Margot Stevenson, Eddie Foy Jr.

Brother Rat and a Baby. (GB: *Baby Be Good*) 1940. Warner Bros. Director: Ray Enright. With Wayne Morris, Priscilla Lane, Eddie Albert, Jane Wyman.

An Angel from Texas. 1940. Warner Bros. Director: Ray Enright. With Eddie Albert, Wayne Morris, Jane Wyman.

Murder in the Air. 1940. Warner Bros. Director: Lewis Seiler. With John Litel, James Stephenson, Eddie Foy Jr.

Knute Rockne – All American. Warner Bros. 1940. Director: Lloyd Bacon. With Pat O'Brien, Gale Page.

Tugboat Annie Sails Again. 1940. Warner Bros. Director: Lewis Seiler. With Marjorie Rambeau, Alan Hale, Jane Wyman.

Santa Fe Trail. 1940. Warner Bros./First National. Director: Michael Curtiz. With Errol Flynn, Olivia de Havilland, Raymond Massey.

The Bad Man. 1941. Metro-Goldwyn-Mayer. Director: Richard Thorpe. With Wallace Beery, Lionel Barrymore, Laraine Day.

Million Dollar Baby. 1941. Warner Bros. Director: Curtis Bernhardt. With Priscilla Lane, Jeffrey Lynn, May Robson.

Nine Lives Are Not Enough. 1941. Warner Bros. Director: A. Edward Sutherland. With Joan Perry, James Gleason.

International Squadron. 1941. Warner Bros. Director: Lothar Mendes. With James Stephenson, Olympe Bradna.

King's Row. 1942. Warner Bros. Director: Sam Wood. With Ann Sheridan, Robert Cummings.

Juke Girl. 1942. Warner Bros. Director: Curtis Bernhardt. With Ann Sheridan, Richard Whorf.

Desperate Journey. 1942. Warner Bros. First National. Director: Raoul Walsh. With Errol Flynn, Raymond Massey, Nancy Coleman.

This Is the Army. 1943. Warner Bros. Director: Michael Curtiz. With George Murphy, Joan Leslie.

Stallion Road. 1947. Warner Bros. Director: James V. Kern. With Alexis Smith, Zachary Scott.

That Hagen Girl. 1947. Warner Bros. Director: Peter Godfrey. With Shirley Temple.

The Voice of the Turtle. 1947. Warner Bros. Director: Irving Rapper. With Eleanor Parker, Eve Arden, Wayne Morris.

John Loves Mary. 1949. Warner Bros. Director: David Butler. With Patricia Neal, Jack Carson, Wayne Morris.

Night unto Night. 1949. Warner Bros. Director: Don Siegel. With Viveca Lindfors.

The Girl from Jones Beach. 1949. Warner Bros. Director: Peter Godfrey. With Virginia Mayo, Eddie Bracken.

It's a Great Feeling. 1949. Warner Bros. Director: David Butler. With Jack Carson, Dennis Morgan, Doris Day.

The Hasty Heart. 1950. Warner Bros. Director: Vincent Sherman. With Richard Todd, Patricia Neal.

Louisa. 1950. Universal. Director: Alexander Hall. With Charles Coburn, Ruth Hussey, Edmund Gwenn, Spring Byington.

Storm Warning. 1951. Warner Bros. Director: Stuart Heisler. With Ginger Rogers, Doris Day.

Bedtime for Bonzo. 1951. Universal. Director: Frederick de Cordova. With Dianna Lynn, Walter Slezak.

The Last Outpost. 1951. Paramount. Director: Lewis R. Foster. With Rhonda Fleming, Bruce Bennett.

Hong Kong. 1952. Paramount. Director: Lewis R. Foster. With Rhonda Fleming, Nigel Bruce, Danny Chang.

She's Working Her Way Through College. 1952. Warner Bros. Director: H. Bruce Humberstone. With Virginia Mayo, Gene Nelson.

The Winning Team. 1952. Warner Bros. Director: Lewis Seiler. With Doris Day, Frank Lovejoy.

Tropic Zone. 1953. Paramount. Director: Lewis R. Foster. With Rhonda Fleming, Estelita, Noah Beery Jr.

Law and Order. 1953. Universal. Director: Nathan Juran. With Dorothy Malone, Alex Nicol.

Prisoner of War. 1954. Metro-Goldwyn-Mayer. Director: Andrew Marton. With Steve Forrest, Dewey Martin.

Cattle Queen of Montana. 1954. RKO. Director: Allan Dwan. With Barbara Stanwyck, Gene Evans.

Tennessee's Partner. 1955. RKO. Director: Allan Dwan. With John Payne, Rhonda Fleming, Coleen Gray.

Hellcats of the Navy. 1957. Columbia. Director: Nathan Juran. With Nancy Davis, Arthur Franz.

The Killers. 1964. NBC-TV. Director: Don Siegel. With Lee Marvin, John Cassavetes, Angie Dickinson.